Holding Nothing Back

TIM HUGHES

Regal

From Gospel Light
Ventura, California, U.S.A.

Published by Regal Books
From Gospel Light
Ventura, California, U.S.A.

Internal design by joshuatalbotdesign.com

Library of Congress Cataloging-in-Publication Data
Hughes, Tim, 1977-
  Holding nothing back / Tim Hughes.
    p. cm.
  ISBN 978-0-8307-4282-0 (trade paper)
  1. God—Worship and love. 2. Worship. I. Title.
  BV4817.H84 2007
  231'.6—dc22   2007012390

105453881

Rights for publishing this book in other languages are contracted by Gospel Light Worldwide, the international
nonprofit ministry of Gospel Light. For additional information, visit www.gospellightworldwide.org.

To my gorgeous wife, Rachel.
Sharing this life with you is my greatest joy.
I love you with all my heart.

Chapter 1: You Are Above and Beyond Understanding 06

Chapter 2: You Opened My Eyes to Your Wonders Anew.................... 24

Chapter 3: Creation Joins as One to Sing.................................... 36

Chapter 4: When Silence Falls 48

Chapter 5: You'll Be the Song in My Heart................................... 60

Chapter 6: I Am Yours, Jesus, You Are Mine.................................72

Chapter 7: Living for Your Glory... 84

Chapter 8: Christ in Me, the Hope of Glory 96

Closing Thoughts: Holding Nothing Back.....................................108

Chapter Notes... 112

You Are Above and Beyond Understanding

CHAPTER 1

We all crowded together in a small room. Expectant and excited for a day of input and teaching, we eagerly waited for the first session to start, then as the worship leader picked up his guitar, we all stood—obedient and well-trained churchgoers—and waited to be led.

Eyes closed and emotively strumming on his guitar, clearly already in the zone, the worship leader began singing out: "How are You doing today, God? What's on Your mind? What's consuming Your thoughts? Are You worried about anything today, God? What's getting You down?" This was definitely different from most of the calls to worship I had been involved in.

Caught in this moment, our worship leader friend carried on: "What are You up to today, God? Are You looking after the starving child in Africa, or are You helping the stressed-out mum find her car keys so she can get her kids to school on time?" At this we all began to look at each other, somewhat puzzled and perplexed.

I'll be honest—it was not the greatest start to a worship time. Rather than being filled with awe and amazement at the strength and might of the Sovereign Lord, I began to panic that He might be having a crisis of confidence. Maybe God needed a rest, some time out. I mean, He has been going at it full-tilt for quite a while now.

Before this line of thinking spun out of control, I stopped myself and thought, *Isn't God everywhere? Isn't He all-powerful? Isn't He eternal? Isn't He all-knowing and unchanging?* In our time of worship, we were dumbing God down to our earthly level, trying to relate to Him as "our good old mate 'round the corner." We had forgotten the *otherness* of God. He is transcendent and glorious, above and beyond understanding.

A. W. Tozer, in his classic book *The Knowledge of the Holy*, wrote, "The Church has surrendered her once lofty concept of God and has substituted for it one so low, so ignoble as to be utterly unworthy of thinking, worshiping men."[1]

The Church needs to recapture a big picture of all that God is. Our view and understanding of Him will have a significant impact on our worship. As Graham Kendrick says, "Worship is a response and will grow or shrink in direct proportion to our view of Him." So, let us dig a bit deeper and press on into the mystery and character of God.

*   *   *

It was one of the most majestic and terrifying sights I'd ever seen: About 10 meters (30 feet) from our car was a large pride of lions, lying out in the blazing African sun. My heart was beating hard and perspiration was beginning to pour down my face. After a couple of minutes, I was keen to move on. *Really* keen to move on!

Unfortunately for me I happened to be sharing a 4 x 4 with an overzealous photographer! It soon became apparent that a few snaps out of the window just weren't going to suffice, so before long he was climbing onto the roof and asking the driver to rev the engine in the hope that the lions might start moving—not something I was very keen to see happen!

As one of the lions rose to its feet and stared in our direction, never have I felt so small and vulnerable. This magnificent animal stood there utterly fearless. Looking back, I was so glad we stayed, but at the time I was hugely relieved when we moved on.

In Hosea, there is a verse that on first read seems very strange: "They will follow the LORD; He will roar like a lion. When he roars, his children will come trembling from the west" (Hos. 11:10). In most scenarios when a lion roars, all run for cover. No one in their right mind messes about with a roaring lion. Yet in this picture we see God described as a lion—ferocious, powerful and kingly—and when He roars, His children come running toward Him. What a stunning picture: the weakness, fragility and innocence of a child running toward the thing that should terrify and overwhelm him. But God's children do not draw near casually. Trembling, they run reverently toward this great God. His roar is overpowering, intimidating and spectacular, but as they hear it, they must run toward Him. Humbly, respectfully and mindfully they draw close. He terrifies, yet welcomes in.

St. Augustine wrote about the moment when for the first time he saw closely the mystery of God. He trembled "for love and in terror" and the thought of God made him at once "shiver and burn with desire."[2] The psalmist writes, "You alone are to be feared. Who can stand before you when you are angry?" (Ps. 76:7), yet later we read, "The LORD is gracious and compassionate, slow to anger and rich in love. The LORD is good to all; he has compassion on all he had made" (Ps. 145:8-9).

We need to embrace these two sides of God, the friendship and the fear. As Paul exhorts us in the book of Romans, "Consider therefore the kindness and the sternness of God" (11:22). In the same way we need two eyes in order to enjoy any perception of depth and distance, we also need to grasp these two aspects of God's character to greater understand Him, and ultimately fall more in love with Him.

It is important to remember that God is not made in our image. On the contrary, we are made in His. "For I am God and not man—the Holy One among you" (Hos. 11:9).

There are many attributes to God's character that we can imitate. We can be loving, we can be faithful, we can be forgiving, we can be good and we can be comforting. However, there are certain aspects of God's nature that we as human beings simply cannot share in, qualities in His character that show Him to be totally *other*. These incommunicable attributes set Him apart as God and remind us that we are merely mortal. As Wayne Grudem writes:

> The difference between God's being and ours is more than the difference between the sun and a candle, more than the difference between the ocean and a raindrop, more than the difference between the Artic ice cap and a snowflake, more than the difference between the universe and the room we are sitting in: God's being is qualitatively different. No limitation or imperfection in creation should be projected on to our thought of God. He is the creator; all else is creaturely. All else can pass away in an instant; he necessarily exists forever.[3]

*   *   *

As humans, we need many things to happen on a daily basis in order to survive. We need a constant oxygen supply and a regular source of water, as well as certain proteins, vitamins and nutrients. Every one of us possesses an armory of instincts that keep us alive. If we're too cold, we find shelter and warmth. If we're in pain, we seek help and a cure.

As humans we're a pretty needy bunch. Within a few hours of birth, many animals are not only feeding but are also standing up and walking around. By comparison, human babies are somewhat pathetic—their only way to survive is by screaming. Babies alter both the pitch and volume of their cry depending on how urgent their need of help. The louder and more piercing the scream, the quicker the response. In this way a human baby gets all the care and attention it needs to survive.

God does not need us or anything in creation in order to survive and exist. He's the uncreated God, absolutely independent and self-sufficient.

> Before the mountains were born
> or you brought forth the earth and the world,
> from everlasting to everlasting you are God
> (Ps. 90:2).

> The God who made the world and everything in it is the Lord of heaven and earth and does not live in temples built by hands. And he is not served by human hands, as if he needed anything, because he himself gives all men life and breath and everything else (Acts 17:24-25).

> For every animal in the forest is mine,
> and the cattle on a thousand hills.
> I know every bird in the mountains,
> and the creatures of the field are mine.
> If I were hungry I would not tell you,
> for the world is mine and all that is in it
> (Ps. 50:10-12).

These verses put a lot into perspective. Our God does not need us in order to survive and exist, but as His creation we can bring Him enormous joy and pleasure. He is not reliant upon us, yet He deeply desires our affection and intimacy. He did not need to create us, but He freely chose to do so.

He is complete without us, but He chooses to draw near and befriend us. What an amazing God!

* * *

Nothing on Earth is permanent. Over the years, air, land and sea alter, and living things adapt as best they can. Humans change. We may not like it, but change is impossible to escape.

Every second, more than 2 million red blood cells are destroyed in the human body.[4] During a 24-hour period, the average human will breathe approximately 23,000 times.[5] Your ears and nose continue to grow throughout your entire life. We grow old; we gradually wear out.

Around us, the earth's boundaries are in a perpetual flux of change as erosion runs its course. As global warming wreaks havoc—tsunamis, flooding, drought and hurricanes—the rate and violence of change is increased exponentially. In America, the San Andreas Fault, which runs from north to south, is slipping at a rate of about 5 centimeters per year, causing Los Angeles to move toward San Francisco. Scientists forecast that Los Angeles will be a suburb of the city of San Francisco in about 15 million years.[6]

But change is not just physical. Our feelings can turn in the blink of an eye. The heroes of yesterday become the villains of today.

People fall in and out of love at an alarming rate. I think of a friend of mine whose life was ripped apart one day when his wife came home to say, "I don't love you anymore." I have felt the personal pain of breakdown in relationships—the smiles and pats on the back replaced by aloofness and silence. The wear and tear of life leaves us crushed and exhausted. Our existence becomes guarded and we are cautious to give freely of ourselves.

What a relief it is to center our lives around a God who is unchanging. A God who is faithful to the end and whose promises are secure. A God who will never leave nor forsake us. A God who can't lie to us. A God who will never let us go.

> In the beginning you laid the foundations of the earth
> and the heavens are the work of your hands.
> They will perish, but you remain;
> they will all wear out like a garment.
> Like clothing you will change them
> and they will be discarded.
> But you remain the same, and your years never end
> (Ps. 102:25-27).

> God is not man that he should lie, nor a son of man, that he should change his mind. Does he speak and then not act? Does he promise and then not fulfil? (Num. 23:19).

> For I the LORD do not change (Mal. 3:6).

We have all experienced the searing pain of loss in some shape or form. We have been wounded by the reality of change, by a breakdown in relationship, the loss of a loved one or the end of a dream. In the midst of such uncertainty, we can look to a steadfast God who never changes like shifting shadows, who will never fall in and out of love with us. We are His for eternity. Our names are written on His hand. As Grudem says, "Our faith and hope and knowledge all ultimately depend on a person who is infinitely worthy of trust—because He is absolutely and eternally unchanging in his being, perfections, purposes and promises."[7]

*   *   *

God has no beginning and end. He didn't suddenly begin to exist. He always was. Alpha and Omega, He will never die. He is the God who was and is and is to come.

> The number of His years is unsearchable (Job 36:26, *NASB*).

> To the only God, our Savior through Jesus Christ our Lord, be glory, majesty, dominion, and authority, before all time and now and forever. Amen (Jude 25, *NASB*).

> With the Lord a day is like a thousand years, and a thousand years is like a day (2 Pet. 3:8).

Do we have an eternal perspective? Trying to comprehend something that never ends is overwhelming. Everything we know on this earth has a beginning and an end. We are born; we die. We wake up; we go to sleep. God alone is eternal and we could spend a lifetime trying to fathom this incomprehensible truth. As we look to this God whose years are limitless, whose days are unending, we are reminded that we worship a truly vast and glorious God. When human touches God, the finite touches the infinite.

While we struggle through this earthly life, we know that one day we will find everlasting joy as we worship the God of eternity face to face.

> Brief life is here our portion,
> Brief sorrow, short lived care;
> The life that knows no ending,
> The tearless life is there.
> There God, our King and Portion,
> In fullness of His grace,
> We then shall see forever,
> And worship face to face.[8]

*   *   *

All around us, God is present. We cannot escape Him. He is present at every point of space. He is unrestricted by size or spatial dimensions. God cannot be contained or limited. He is everywhere.

> "Am I only a God nearby," declares the LORD, "and not far away? Can anyone hide in secret places so that I can't see him?" declares the LORD. "Do not I fill heaven and earth?" declares the LORD (Jer. 23:23-24).

> Where can I go from your Spirit?
> Where can I flee from your presence?
> If I go up to the heavens you are there;

if I make my bed in the depths, you are there.
If I rise on the wings of the dawn,
if I settle on the far side of the sea,
even there your hand will guide me,
your right hand will hold me fast
(Ps. 139:7-10).

But will God indeed dwell on the earth? Behold, heaven and
the highest heaven cannot contain you; how much less this
house which I have built? (1 Kings 8:27).

Growing up, one of my dad's favorite phrases was "I've only got two hands." The great news is that God has all the hands! He can do all things. Turning His attention to one person in need does not mean He has no time to listen to our cries for help. It is never either/or. We are limited, restricted by time. For us there really are never enough hours in the day. Wonderfully, God is not like us.

*   *   *

Robert Webber writes, "Worship needs to acknowledge the unknowable nature of God who is transcendent and other and dwells in eternal mystery."[9] There are many other aspects of God's character that we could explore, revealing His divine transcendent nature. He is omniscient, meaning that He is all-knowing, perfect in knowledge. He is omnipotent, meaning that He is all-powerful. He has an "incomprehensible plenitude of power."[10]

We could spend a lifetime studying these attributes and still we will only know in part. We could use every word in the dictionary to describe the character of God and yet we would fail to even come close to doing Him justice. I leave you with these rich and wonderful words from Dr. S. M. Lockridge:

> He's the King of Righteousness.
> He's the King of the Ages.
> He's the King of Heaven.
> He's the King of Glory.
> He's the King of kings and He's the Lord of lords.
> That's my King.
>
> Well, I wonder do you know Him.
>
> My King is a sovereign King.
> No means of measure can define His limitless love.
> No far seeing telescope can bring into visibility the coastline of His shoreless supply.
> No barrier can hinder Him from pouring out His blessings.
>
> He's enduringly strong
> He's entirely sincere
> He's eternally steadfast
> He's immortally graceful
> He's imperially powerful
> He's impartially merciful

Do you know Him?

He's the greatest phenomenon that has ever crossed the
horizon of this world.
He's God's Son.

He's the sinner's Savior.

He's unique
He's unparalleled
He's unprecedented
He's the loftiest idea in literature
He's the highest personality in philosophy

He supplies strength for the weak.
He's available for the tempted and the tried.
He sympathizes and He saves.
He strengthens and sustains.
He guards and He guides.
He heals the sick.
He cleansed the lepers.
He forgives sinners.
He discharges debtors.
He delivers the captive.
His promise is sure.
His life is matchless.

His goodness is limitless.
His mercy is everlasting.
His love never changes.
His Word is enough.
His grace is sufficient.
His reign is righteous and
His yoke is easy and
His burden is light.

I wish I could describe Him to you.
But He's *indescribable*!!![11]

You Opened My Eyes to Your Wonders Anew

CHAPTER 2

every Wednesday we had gathered together to unpack life's biggest questions. During the Alpha Course we had shared our deepest fears and our greatest longings. We had journeyed together and seen some wonderful highs and desperate lows.

One of the members of the group had encountered God for the first time in an amazing way, and his world had been turned upside down. It only seemed right to ask him to close our final time together in prayer. His prayer was one of the most stunning things I have ever heard. This brand-new Christian prayed, "God, thank You for being with us. You've met with us in incredible ways. And, Jesus, thank You that one day I will see You face to face. And I cannot wait. I cannot wait! Amen." At this he broke down in tears, a successful, intellectual city accountant, reduced to tears at his new understanding of God's unceasing love.[1]

We love because He first loved us. As Paul says in Romans:

> Therefore, I urge you, brothers, in view of God's mercy, to offer your bodies as living sacrifices, holy and pleasing to God—this is your spiritual act of worship (12:1).

It is *in view of God's mercy* that we offer up our bodies. Throughout the Bible it is amazing to see how God reveals Himself to different individuals. Uncreated, all-powerful, self-existent, Maker of all things, far above understanding, uncontained, unbreakable, infinite God, meeting small, finite, but-a-breath human. It is not much of a match. Yet time and again we see God reach out His mighty hand to save, encourage, inspire, affirm, challenge

One of my favorite God encounters in the Bible is Moses at the burning bush. On the far side of the desert, in the middle of nowhere, Moses wandered around tending to his father-in-law's sheep. In this mundane moment, Moses suddenly saw an unusual sight that caught his eye: A burning bush—nothing out of the ordinary in the dry heat of the desert, hardly the event of the century—but there was something different about this burning bush. It kept on burning and burning and burning without actually burning up! This phenomenon was so fascinating that Moses was captivated and decided to investigate further. "I will now turn aside and see this great sight, why the bush does not burn" (Exod. 3:3, *KJV*). In that moment, beside that burning bush, Moses encountered God and was changed forever. He was consumed by the glory of God.

God is glorious. He is so spectacularly beautiful and majestic that when we catch the smallest of glimpses, we too are captivated. We are forever changed, left undone and lost in wonder. We respond to the overwhelming revelation of an incomprehensible God.

Wonder is the basis of worship. Scottish historian Thomas Carlyle once said, "The man who cannot wonder, who does not habitually wonder and worship, is but a pair of spectacles behind which there is no eye." As we step aside to inquire more into the mystery and awe of who God is, our hearts are captured. The more we look, the more we find. If you look at the night sky, you can count approximately 3,000 stars with your naked eye. Look through binoculars, and you can see thousands more. But if you look through a powerful telescope, you can see stars in the billions. As we wait, ponder and muse, we will always discover more of God.

A few years ago I was on holiday in Australia with a friend. One morning I was reading my Bible when a verse jumped out at me: "He had no beauty or majesty to attract us to him, nothing in his appearance that we should desire him" (Isa. 53:2). Thinking I had misread the verse, I scanned over the words again. Is that correct? Did Jesus, the Son of God, walk upon the earth, displaying no beauty or majesty that would attract us to Him?

In Philippians we read that Jesus "made himself nothing, taking the very nature of a servant, being made in human likeness" (Phil. 2:7). What humility. What sacrifice. The King of the universe chose to take on the status of a slave and walked upon the earth as man. If we were to have passed Him by, there was nothing about Him physically that would have caused us to take a second look. And yet Jesus' appeal drew huge crowds, His presence alone was utterly attractive to human beings, and His magnetism forces us to refine our preconceptions about beauty. For those of us whose eyes have glimpsed the beauty of Christ, we are forever captivated. Like Moses at the burning bush, we are left transfixed, overwhelmed by such a sight—and our response is worship.

It was out of this revelation that I wrote the song "Beautiful One."

> You opened my eyes to Your wonders anew
> You captured my heart with this love
> Because nothing on Earth is as beautiful as You.[2]

* * *

As a result of his determination to spread the word of God, John was imprisoned on the island of Patmos. One day, "in the Spirit," he heard a voice from behind him. Turning around to find the source of the voice, he saw a sight that caused his body to fall to the floor as though dead. Such was the physical magnitude of this vision that John was unable to take it in.

Awestruck, he struggled later to find the right words to describe all that he had seen—everything was "like" something else. Someone "like a son of man," His head and hair were white "like" wool, His eyes were "like" blazing fire and His voice was "like" the sound of rushing waters. As John lay at His feet, completely dumbfounded, this extraordinary figure placed the same right hand that held seven stars on John saying, "Do not be afraid. I am the First and the Last. I am the Living One; I was dead, and behold I am alive for ever and ever!" (Rev. 1:17-18). That day John encountered the Lord God Almighty, Jesus Christ.

As the vision unfolds, John journeys to the·throne in heaven, the Holy of Holies. Here we are privileged to catch a glimpse of the worship of heaven:

> In the center, around the throne, were four living creatures, and they were covered with eyes, in front and in back. The first living creature was like a lion, the second was like an ox, the third had a face like a man, the fourth was like a flying eagle. Each of the four living creatures had six wings and was covered with eyes all around, even under his wings. Day and night they never stop saying: "Holy, holy, holy is the Lord God Almighty, who was, and is, and is to come." Whenever the living creatures give glory, honor and thanks to him who sits on the throne and who lives for ever and ever, the twenty-four elders fall down before him who sits on the throne, and worship him who lives for ever and ever. They lay their crowns

before the throne and say: "You are worthy, our Lord and God, to receive glory and honor and power, for you created all things, and by your will they were created and have their being" (Rev. 4:6-11).

What an incredible sight these four living creatures must have been, covered in eyes in front and in back! I have often wondered why they have so many eyes . . . perhaps it is in order to better see and take in the wonder of God? As they catch sight of the One seated on the Throne, they cry, "Holy, holy, holy is the Lord God Almighty, who was, and is, and is to come." Amazing—day and night they never stop saying it. Even now as you read through these words, they are at it. "Holy, holy, holy . . ."

Tonight, when your head hits the pillow and you fall asleep, they will continue, "Holy, holy, holy . . ." I sometimes imagine them beginning to flag— I mean, it must get pretty exhausting! As they tire they catch another glimpse of the Great I Am and their hearts sore with praise, "Holy, holy, holy . . ." Every fresh revelation, every different angle, every moment of insight fuels the praise of heaven.

As all this goes on, the 24 elders join in. While the living creatures give glory and honor and thanks, the 24 elders fall down before Him who sits on the throne and they worship. They cast their crowns before such greatness and say, "You are worthy, our Lord and God, to receive glory and honor and power, for you created all things, and by your will they were created and have their being."

This perpetual worship goes on all around us. It never stops. The heavens never become exhausted of worshiping. It doesn't become monotonous or predictable. It simply goes on and on and on. Just think about that for a

moment. The God we worship is so unbelievably astounding, resplendent, powerful and majestic, that for all of eternity, we will never grow weary of worshiping Him.

It is interesting to note the pattern of worship in Revelation: The worshipers *recognize* and then *respond*. As they get caught up in responding and pouring out praise, they recognize more. As they recognize more, they respond with even greater vigor and passion. The process of recognizing and responding never ends, and one day we too will be drawn up to join the hosts of heaven praising forever. For now we see in part, but one day we will see face to face (see 1 Cor. 13:12). What a glorious day!

* * *

God reveals Himself as all-powerful and holy, but He also discloses Himself as merciful and kind. One of my favorite "Jesus stories" in the Bible is the one about the woman caught in adultery. I can picture the scene: This probably half-naked and utterly terrified woman was dragged by the religious leaders through the town and into the temple where Jesus was standing. She had been caught red-handed having sex with a man that was not her husband and dragged from the "scene of the crime." She'd probably already taken a few hits and knew very well what was coming: At that time, adultery was one of the worst things a woman could do, and the punishment was death by stoning.

Every one of those religious leaders had their eyes fixed on Jesus, waiting to see what He would do. They probably had their stones in their hands, ready to kill. But in that moment, Jesus did something totally unexpected. He thought for a moment, and then said, "If any one of you is without sin, let him be the first to throw a stone at her" (John 8:7).

I bet you could have cut the atmosphere with a knife. The woman stood there shaking with fear, and the leaders stood there not knowing what to do next—and all the while Jesus waited, strong and just.

One by one, the leaders dropped their rocks and walked away. When they had all gone away, Jesus looked straight into the woman's eyes and asked if there was anyone left to convict her.

"No one, sir," she replied.

"Then neither do I condemn you. Go now and leave your life of sin..." (John 8:11).

The woman expected to find judgment, but instead, in the eyes of Jesus, she found mercy. As she encountered the kindness of God, she was moved to repentance. From that day on, she was never again the same.

*   *   *

I was sitting at the back of the church, minding my own business, and as I looked out and watched people worshiping, I noticed a few enthusiasts at the front waving brightly colored flags. I remember telling myself that I'd never do anything like that—flag-waving was not for me.

My heart skipped a beat as I sensed God prompting me to respond to Him in worship by waving a flag. At first I laughed it off, thinking it was my mind playing tricks, but gradually I came to a conviction that it was the Lord speaking. I wrestled for a while, pleading with God not to make me to do it—but we were singing, "I'll bring you more than a song, for a song in itself is not what you have required."[3] I knew what I had to do.

Leaving my seat, I walked to the front, picked up one of the less-brightly colored flags and started to wave it. I could feel the eyes of all my friends burning in the back of my head. As I waved that flag, something inside me died, but my worship came alive. I never want my pride or fear of what people think about me to get in the way of God encounters like that one.

Worship should be all-consuming. When our eyes our open to see the greatness and the kindness of our God, we should respond with every fiber of our being. As John Piper writes:

> If God's reality is displayed to us in His Word, and we do not then feel in our heart any grief or longing or hope or fear or awe or joy or confidence, then we may dutifully sing and pray and recite and gesture as much as we like, but it will not be real worship. We cannot honour God if our hearts are far from Him. The engagement of the heart in worship is the coming alive of the feelings and emotions and affections of the heart. Where feelings for God are dead, worship is dead.[4]

It should be common in our churches to see people weeping in worship, overwhelmed by the depth of God's mercy. It should be common to see people dancing like lunatics, free and abandoned before their Maker. It should be common to be overcome by the enormous volume of people singing and shouting praise at the tops of their voices. It should be common to see people lost in silence, no one wanting to move, totally transfixed by the transcendence of God.

Recently a friend of mine e-mailed me about a time of worship he had been involved in. He described it, saying it was "as much of heaven as a human can take without exploding!" What a great definition of worship.

John Stott writes, "There is something fundamentally flawed about a purely academic interest in God. God is not an appropriate object for cool, critical, detached, scientific observation. No, the true knowledge of God will always lead us to worship, as it did Paul. Our place is on our faces before Him in adoration."[5]

As we delve into His Word, as we behold His glory spectacularly displayed throughout creation, as we reverently draw near to God, His wonderful promise is that He will draw near to us. Beholding His beauty, we are left forever undone.

To know God is to love God.

Creation Joins as one to Sing

CHAPTER 3

Still your heart. Quiet your soul. Turn the radio off. Step outside and allow yourself to tune in. Can you hear the sound? The wind rushing through the trees, the waves lapping against the shore, the birds filling the air with melody. Creation alive in song, responding to its Creator.

St. Paul's Cathedral overlooks the city of London and remains one of its most famous and stunning landmarks. The cathedral, completed in 1710, was the work of the architect Sir Christopher Wren, and is considered a true masterpiece. Search throughout the cathedral, however, and you will find no memorial to its designer. Rather, there is an inscription over the north door that reads: "If you are looking for a memorial, look around you." The celebration of Sir Christopher Wren's accomplishment is not a grand plaque or ostentatious statue, but *what he built*—the architecture speaks for itself. In the same way, creation surrounds us, full of beauty and wonder, revealing the greatness of its Creator.

The medieval philosopher and theologian, Bonaventura, put it like this:

> All creatures of this sensible world lead the soul of the wise and contemplative person to the eternal God, since they are the shadows, echoes and pictures, the vestiges, images and manifestations of that most powerful, most wise and best first principle, of that eternal origin, light and fullness, of that productive, exemplary and order-giving Art. They are set before us for the sake of our knowing God, and are divinely given signs. For every creature is by its very nature a kind of portrayal and likeness of that eternal Wisdom.[1]

We need to take time and stop to consider God's wonders (see Job 37:14). The universe around us is God's breathtaking masterpiece. Consider the silent beauty of the stars: Human empires rise and fall, yet the star-studded heavens continue to shine, majestic and glorious. Recently I read about a collection of stars known as neutron stars, which are actually quite small (for stars), often measuring no more than 10 miles across. Unbelievably though, one teaspoon of a neutron star's matter weighs *three billion tons*. If a small piece of neutron star dropped onto the ground, it would slice through the earth like a bullet through cotton.[2]

Consider the dimensions of space. We live in a vast universe. If we could travel in a space shuttle at a speed of 30,000 miles per hour, it would take over 85,000 years to reach the star that is nearest to our sun, the Proxima Centauri. To put that in perspective for you: If our sun was the size of the dot over a letter *i*, the nearest star would be a dot 10 miles away.[3]

Consider the oceans, full of varied and spectacular life. A nearly invisible fish that swims among the icebergs of the Artic and Antarctic oceans manages to survive in these freezing waters due to a special protein that acts like an anti-freeze to keep crystals from forming. With no hemoglobin or red pigment in its blood, it has a ghostly white appearance that makes it appear almost transparent.

Stretching from between 3,000 to 15,000 feet in depth lies the "deep sea." Scientists have only recently begun exploring these depths, and have discovered 500 previously unknown species of marine life. These include a furry crab, a squid that can chew its food, and a shrimp that survives alongside volcanic vents that spew out water heated to 470 degrees Celsius (878° F).

Scientists believe there are plenty more surprises to discover, with an estimated 90 percent of marine life as yet undocumented anywhere in the world.[4] Nature documentary producer Alistair Fothergill says, "We know more about the surface of the moon than the deep oceans of our own planet."[5]

Consider the Grand Canyon, the largest gorge on planet Earth. It stretches 290 miles across the face of the Colorado Plateau in northern Arizona and, rim to rim, measures up to 15 miles across. At the canyon's bottom (an average depth of one mile), the Colorado River cuts through Granite Gorge, exposing some of the oldest rocks visible anywhere on Earth, some nearly two billion years old.[6] John Wesley Powell, an American explorer, once described the sound of rushing water in the canyon as "a symphony of multitudinous melodies."[7]

Consider the intricate design of the human body. One human brain generates more electrical impulses in a single day than the world's telephones put together. In one square inch of skin there lie 4 yards of nerve fibers, 1,300 nerve cells, 100 sweat glands, 3 million cells and 3 yards of blood vessels. The average human heart will beat 3,000 million times in its lifetime and pump 48 million gallons of blood. The human thighbone is stronger than concrete.[8] Whether you feel it or not, our human bodies are exceptional masterpieces, perfectly designed to hold together and perform.

The starlit heavens, the oceans below, the mountain heights, every creature great and small, have all been made for a purpose: to declare the glory of God and proclaim the works of His hands (see Ps. 19:1). Day and night, they join together to sing a symphony of praise.

*   *   *

The song of creation can be found throughout the Scriptures. In Job, we hear the Lord ask (rhetorically), "Who laid [the earth's] cornerstone while morning stars sang together and all the angels shouted for joy?" (38:6-7). As creation was breathed into being, the stars joined together, singing as one, to respond to their Creator.

In the psalms we read of the seas lifting up their voices (see 93:3). Could it be that every ocean wave that crashes to the shore is a roar of praise offered up to the Maker of all things? Later we catch a powerful image of creation and mankind joining together in worship:

> Shout for joy to the LORD, all the earth, burst into jubilant song with music; make music to the LORD with the harp, with the harp and the sound of singing, with trumpets and the blast of the ram's horn—shout for joy before the LORD, the King. Let the sea resound, and everything in it, the world and all who live in it. Let the rivers clap their hands, let the mountains sing together for joy (Ps. 98:4-8).

What a beautiful image: the music of our harps, trumpets, drums, guitars and voices joining with the resounding cheer of the seas, mountains and rivers. This song of creation goes on all around us, demonstrating the glory and greatness of our God.

In Isaiah we find these verses:

> You will go out in joy and be led forth in peace;
> the mountains and hills burst into song before you
> and the trees of the field will clap their hands (55:12).

High heavens, sing! God has done it.
Deep earth, shout! And you mountains sing!
A forest choir of oaks and pines and cedars!
God has redeemed Jacob.
God's glory is on display in Israel (44:23, *THE MESSAGE*).

In C. S. Lewis's *The Magicians Nephew*, we read a beautiful passage of Aslan, the great lion creating the Narnian world through song. A boy from our world, Digory, experiences the wonder:

In the darkness something was happening at last. A voice had begun to sing. It was very far away and Digory found it hard to decide from what direction it was coming. Sometimes it seemed to come from all directions at once. Sometimes he almost thought it was coming out of the earth beneath them. Its lower notes were deep enough to be the voice of the earth herself. There were no words. There was hardly even a tune. But it was, beyond comparison, the most beautiful noise he had ever heard. It was so beautiful he could hardly bear it . . .

Then two wonders happened at the same moment. One was that the voice was suddenly joined by other voices; more voices than you could possibly count. They were in harmony with it, but far higher up the scale: cold, tingling, silvery voices. The second wonder was that the blackness overhead, all at once, was blazing with stars. They didn't come out gently one by one, as they do on a summer evening.

One moment there had been nothing but darkness; next moment a thousand, thousand points of light leapt out— single stars, constellations, and planets, brighter and bigger than any in our world. There were no clouds. The stars and the new voices began at exactly the same time. If you'd seen and heard it, as Digory did, you would have seemed quite certain that it was the stars themselves which were singing, and it was the First Voice, the deep one, which had made them appear and made them sing.[9]

As we listen to creation's song, we are moved to fall more in love with the Creator. Theologian Alister McGrath writes, "It is part of the purpose of the creator that we should hear the music of the cosmos, and, through loving its harmonies, come to love their composer."[10] Every note, every beat and every sound throughout creation reminds us that there is an infinite God who set the world in motion.

This song of creation isn't simply restricted to the earth, however. We see in the worship that surrounds the throne of God that creation joins with the chorus of heaven to worship the Savior:

Then I heard every creature in heaven and on earth and under the earth and on the sea, and all that is in them singing: "To Him who sits on the throne and to the Lamb be praise and honor and glory and power for ever and ever" (Rev. 5:13).

We have a special role to play in creation's praise. As humans we are called to gather up the praise of creation and put it into words, presenting it before God. As N. T. Wright says, "To take the inanimate and seemingly inarticulate praise of creation," and give it a voice.[11] We see this in the worship of heaven. As we saw in the previous chapter, the many-eyed creatures cry, "Holy, holy, holy, is the Lord God Almighty," but it is the 24 elders who give reason for their praise: "You are worthy . . . *for you* created all things, and by your will they were created and have their being" (Rev. 4:11, emphasis added). The human elders give glory and honor because they have minds to understand why God is so worthy.

Rather than just "doing worship" as creation does, we humans are given the task of discerning *why* we should worship. We then have a choice to voice creation's praise, or ignore it. Each time we worship, we are enabling creation to praise God.

Graham Kendrick and Paul Baloche express this wonderfully in their song "Creation's King":

> All creation is a song, waiting to be sung
> All of nature like a prayer, waiting for a tongue
> For who will give it voice
> And make its anthem ring
>
> Or rise to lead a choir of all created things?
> Lord hear your people sing[12]

This adds an exciting new dynamic to our corporate times of sung worship—we are speaking and singing on behalf of the whole of creation, joining as one to worship the God who truly is worthy of all praise. When we gather as the Church, we are involved in something so much bigger than simply singing a few worship tunes. We are expressing creation's praise. We are the voice of the trees, the mountains, the oceans, the skies, the whole of creation. The psalmist captures this delightfully:

> Praise him, sun and moon,
> Praise him, all you shining stars . . .
> Praise the LORD from the earth,
> You great sea creatures and all ocean depths,
> Lightening and hail, snow and clouds,
> Stormy winds that do his bidding,
> You mountains and all hills,
> Fruit trees and all cedars,
> Wild animals and all cattle,
> Small creatures and flying birds
> (Ps. 148:3,7-10).

We will never run out of songs to sing—we are caught up in an eternal hymn of praise.

*   *   *

Not everyone can hear creation's praise. Sadly, much of the world around us is stuck in a rut, singing the same old boring melody, tuning in to meaningless songs and sounds. When Jesus made His triumphant entrance into Jerusalem, the whole crowd of disciples began joyfully praising God in loud voices, saying, "Blessed is the King who comes in the name of the Lord," and "Peace in heaven and glory in the highest."

Some of the Pharisees in the crowd, riled by this explosion of worship, said to Jesus, "Teacher, rebuke your disciples!"

To this Jesus simply replied, "I tell you, if they keep quiet, the stones will cry out" (Luke 19:37-40). So great is our God that if we as human beings were not to give voice to His fame, the stones would cry out and worship.

We as God's creation have a choice: We can sing our own song, write our own tunes. In the grand scheme of things, this will only ever amount to a pathetic squeak, a momentary out-of-tune note of little significance. On the other hand, we can add our harmonies and melodies to the ceaseless roar of creation, a song so beautiful and haunting that we will never tire of singing along to it.

In the quiet of the night I have occasionally tried to listen in to the song of the stars. I can tell you, I've never heard them sing about me! I've walked through forests and tried to hear the trees clapping their hands. There has never been a spontaneous rapturous applause to celebrate my presence. But creation bursts into song to celebrate the worth of God. When we rightly choose to join in this song, we get caught up in something so much bigger than our own individual lives: We get lost in creation's great song, and forever respond to creation's King.

When Silence Falls

CHAPTER 4

Have you ever sung this song in church?

> He has driven me away and made me walk
> in darkness rather than light;
> indeed he has turned his hand against
> me again and again all day long . . .
> He has broken my teeth with gravel;
> he has trampled me in the dust
> (Lam. 3:2-3,16).

Or what about this one?

> How long, O LORD?
> Will you forget me forever?
> How long will you hide your face from me?
> How long must I wrestle with my thoughts
> and every day have sorrow in my heart?
> (Ps. 13:1-2).

I'm guessing that you probably haven't. Most of the churches I've visited in the last few years rightly sing the songs of celebration, joy, praise and adoration . . . but they seem to miss out the songs of lament. These songs are deemed "unsuitable" or "melancholy." Is it even appropriate to express pain and anger before such a glorious God? I remember hearing one worship leader recall that she had just 25 minutes to lead her congregation in wor-

In an article entitled "The Hidden Hope in Lament," psychologist and professor Dan Allender wrote, "Christians seldom sing in the minor key. We fear the somber; we seem to hold sorrow in low esteem. We seem predisposed to fear lament as a quick slide into doubt and despair, failing to see that doubt and despair are the dark soil that is necessary to grow confidence and joy."[1]

For generations people have chosen to wear their Sunday best to church, a form of respect for the Holy God they worship. While there's something honorable about arriving at church prepared, "dressed up" and ready to meet with God, I wonder if this emphasis has diminished a place for bringing and sharing our worst before God? A quick glance through the psalms and other books in the Bible reveal many songs of pain and lament, cries of despair and suffering continually offered up to God. The theologian Walter Brueggemann comments:

> Nearly one-half of the Psalms are songs of lament and poems of complaint. Something is known to be deeply amiss in Israel's life with God. And Israel is not at all reluctant to voice what is troubling [her] . . . The lament-complaint, perhaps Israel's most characteristic and vigorous mode of faith, introduces us to a "spirituality of protest." That is, Israel boldly recognizes that all is not right in the world. This is against our easy gentile way of denial, pretending in each other's presence and in the presence of God that "all is well" when it is not.[2]

Searching through the Scriptures and exploring the countless offerings that men and women throughout generations poured out before God begs the question: In the Church of today, have we lost the place of lament in our worship?

*   *   *

The world is singing the blues. Our media is awash with images of heart wrenching pain: tsunamis, earthquakes, suicide bombers, riots, murder and abuse. None of us are immune to pain—everybody hurts. I will never forget the devastating sound of a lady at my church screaming at the news that her daughter had just prematurely lost her twin babies. No words could ever describe the depth of torment uttered in her cries and groans. We can all relate because in some way we've all experienced a dark night of the soul, those moments in life when each day seems to be filled with sorrow.

In England, depression is rife. The number of prescriptions for anti-depressants has risen from 9 million in 1991 to 24 million in 2001.[3] These statistics are not unique to England. People everywhere are hurting and desperate. A friend recently asked me, "Is it me, or is everything in life really painful?" Tune in to the radio and the songs that fill the airwaves predominantly address issues of despair, depression, heartbreak, insecurity, loss of identity and hopelessness. In 2003, the number-one selling song at Christmas in the U.K. was "Mad World" by Michael Andrews featuring Gary Jules:

> Hide my head I wanna drown my sorrow
> No tomorrow, no tomorrow
> And I find it kind of funny, I find it kind of sad
> The dreams in which I'm dying are the best I've ever had [4]

At a time of supposed joy and festivities, the song that most connected with people was a song of bleak despair.

A few years ago I wrote a song called "When the Tears Fall." It was written at a time when life for me was hard. I was experiencing the personal pain of a breakdown in a relationship, as well as an acute awareness of the agony some of my family and friends were going through. One Sunday morning, my aunt tragically died very suddenly in front of her whole church congregation—coming to terms with such a grievous blow and seeing the distress of her family was extremely upsetting. On top of this, some close friends were suffering from the hurt and disappointment of numerous miscarriages. My heart was filled with questions and doubt. One evening, sitting alone in a hotel room in Canada and feeling very low, I started pouring out my heart to God. The first line I sang out was, "I've had questions without answers. I've known sorrow, I have known pain."[5]

I looked for a response—how do you follow a line like that? The answer is, look to Jesus. Everyone on this earth experiences pain, heartache, bereavement and illness. The only difference for those who believe Jesus is Lord is that we have a Savior who we can turn and cling to.

> But there's one thing that I'll cling to
> You are faithful, Jesus, You're true.[6]

As I sang out my pain and doubt, my soul found rest. Looking through the song that was taking shape, I thought at first that this was a personal lament just for me, but the more I pondered, the more I realized that this was a song of worship. The sentiment of the song was just as worshipful as "Here I Am to Worship."

There has to be a place for expressing pain in our churches. We need a bigger picture of what worship is. Questioning God doesn't mean we are disobeying Him. Expressing doubt doesn't mean we are lacking faith.

The dictionary definition of "lament" is "to utter grief in outcries: to wail: to mourn: sorrow expressed in cries: a musical composition of like character."[7] We often see lament as a very negative expression, especially when it comes to our relationship with God—lament can be seen as self-pity or even rebellion toward God. This couldn't be farther from the truth. The whole journey of lament involves asking questions and searching for answers, pressing in to the unknown. As Dan Allender says, "A lament uses the language of pain, anger and confusion and moves us towards God."[8] There is actually something beautiful and selfless about lamenting: To cry out over our own pain and brokenness reveals a longing for a touch of God.

There also must be a place to despair over the degradation of the world we live in. Millions die every day of HIV/AIDS. Hundreds of thousands of children are abused and defiled, fatherless and motherless, left to defend for themselves. Communities are ripped apart by war. Injustice is rife. If this doesn't break our hearts and cause us to lament, then there is something seriously warped about our worship. God's heart breaks for the poor, the widow and the orphan. If we long to be more Christlike, then I have no doubt we will find ourselves regularly on our knees weeping over the suffering that goes on in the world we live. As we do this we are drawn closer in to the heart of God.

*   *   *

Some of my favorite worship stories in the Bible involve lament. There is something incredibly moving about the story of Job. Here we see a man—who, in the eyes of the world, had everything—reduced to nothing. Job was a man who feared God, who was blameless and upright. He had a beautiful family, owned large amounts of land and was hugely successful. The Bible says he was the "greatest man among all the people of the East" (Job 1:3). But on one horrendous day, everything fell apart for Job. His cattle and livestock were destroyed, and (most tragically of all) his sons and daughters were killed. Picture the scene: a messenger standing before Job, breaking this catastrophic news. How would you respond?

> At this Job got up and tore his robe and shaved his head.
> Then he fell to the ground in worship (Job 1:20).

What a response. Heartbroken and confused, Job tore his robe and shaved his head, the customary expression of sorrow. He then fell to the ground, surrendered himself to God and worshiped. Job didn't hide his pain from God, but rather brought his pain before his Creator as he fell to the ground. To offer up praise and worship in that moment must have been immensely costly. (How precious it must have been to God!) It is so easy to sing and praise God when everything is going well, but what happens when we sink to the depths?

One of the fascinating aspects of this story is the reaction of Job's three friends. When these men heard of all the troubles that came upon Job, they set out to comfort him:

> When they saw him from a distance, they could hardly recog-
> nize him; they began to weep aloud, and they tore their robes

and sprinkled dust on their heads. Then they sat on the ground with him for seven days and seven nights. No one said a word to him, because they saw how great his suffering was (Job 2:12-13).

We are often uncomfortable with silence. I have seen so many situations where people are offered clichéd responses to the pain they are experiencing:

"God has a reason for it."

"Don't worry . . . God will make it all alright."

"God is pruning you through this situation."

These may be true, but when faced with the harsh reality of sorrow and pain, words are empty. When Job's friends saw the extent of his pain, they were silenced. What could they possibly say to bring comfort? Silence is a gift from God—at times, it conveys all that words fail to express.

My friend Mike Pilavachi and I have often led evenings of lament at different churches. The response at times has been overwhelming. In these evenings, we worship through song, we delve into the subject, unpack the Scriptures and then we allow people to respond. Many flood to the front to acknowledge their doubt and sorrow.

Some stand, some kneel, many weep. Then we invite others to come and lay a hand on a shoulder or to simply kneel next to someone. This is not a time for words. This is not a time to try and answer questions. This is a time to weep with those who weep. These evenings have been intensely moving, amazing, God-centered nights of worship. Through talking to people afterward, it is clear that for many, the opportunity to express their lament has been a lifeline in their relationship with God. It has opened my own eyes in a new way to the character and nature of God. Rather than hindering our worship, the expression of lament has fueled it.

Expressing anger and pain to God is a beautiful and intimate act. Again Dan Allender says:

> To sing a lament against God in worship reveals far, far greater trust than to sing a jingle about how happy we are and how much we trust him. That kind of song is much like the smiling salesman who meets you with a "Hey, how are ya. You're looking good today; how can I help ya." Lament cuts through insincerity, strips pretence and reveals the raw nerve of trust that angrily approaches the throne of grace and then kneels in awed, robust wonder.[9]

In our everyday lives, the people that we are most likely to share our deepest fears and hurts with are those we love and trust the most. True intimacy can be experienced when we choose to share honestly and vulnerably.

*   *   *

If we return to the songs quoted at the start of this chapter, we see that they don't end where I've left them. There is a journey from complaint and petition to a declaration of praise. A movement from despair to faith. Likewise, in the book of Lamentations, the bitter cries end with words of hope and trust:

Yet this I call to mind and therefore I have hope: Because of the LORD's great love we are not consumed for his compassions

never fail. They are new every morning; great is your faithfulness
(Lam. 3:22-23).

In the psalms, feelings of abandonment and sorrow are followed by singing:

But I trust in your unfailing love;
my heart rejoices in your salvation.
I will sing to the LORD,
for he has been good to me
(Ps. 13:5-6).

It is easy to praise when everything is going to plan. It is more of a challenge when everything around us is falling apart. It takes great faith to say when life is incredibly hard, "You are good." But this is the deal: God is good and is forever worthy of our praise. His worth is not dependent on our feelings. Day and night, always the same, God deserves our highest praise.

Keeping God at the center of our worship enables us to face life's most difficult trials. I think we can find great comfort and healing in the Church if we admit our questions and doubts, yet choose to trust and praise God in the midst of them. As we lift our eyes up off ourselves and fix them on Jesus, our healer, our savior, our defender, our provider, we will find hope and joy. Then we will realize that we always have a song in our hearts to sing.

You'll Be the Song in My Heart

CHAPTER 5

In 1977, on the eve of the launches of American spacecraft Voyager 1 and Voyager 2 into the depths of space, a committee of experts gathered to answer the following question: "How can you make an alien inhabitant of a planet belonging to a distant star system understand what it is like to be a human being on planet Earth?"

To many people's surprise, the experts' answer to this strange question was *music*. They devoted 87.5 minutes of the Voyager video message discs to a selection of "Earth's greatest hits" because the experts thought that music expresses human feelings better than any other medium known to man.

There has never been a society without its own distinctive sound and music to express sadness and pain, as well as joy and elation. Taking a varied selection of Earth's music, a gold-plated copper disc was made, featuring sounds of the didgeridoo played by the Aborigines of Australia, the bamboo flutes of Japan, classical pieces by Beethoven, Bach and Mozart, as well as Chuck Berry screaming out "Johnny B. Goode." Built to last for up to one billion years, the disc took "LP" to a new level![1]

Music is glorious. Did you know that most toilets flush in the key of E-flat?[2] Perhaps more fascinating, it has been proven that cows produce more milk and chickens lay more eggs when listening to pop music.[3] (If you love your cheese omelets, be thankful for Britney Spears!) Thomas Carlyle once said, "Music is well said to be the speech of angels; in fact nothing among the utterances allowed to man is felt to be so divine. It brings us near to the infinite."[4]

Music has the capacity to tap into human emotions like nothing else. Beethoven once remarked, "Music should strike fire from the heart of man and bring tears from the eyes of women."[5] Imagine a movie without a soundtrack, or a party without a sound system, or a restaurant without a musical atmosphere. Music plays a crucial role in our lives. There have been countless moments in my life—driving alone late at night, sitting sleepless on a plane, worshiping at church—where a song has been played that has left me speechless and overwhelmed, reduced to tears or left feeling invincible.

Music is mysterious. It can be so hard to define "great music." What one person loves, another hates. Maybe this explains why musicians throughout generations have had a dislike for music critics. As someone once remarked, "Asking a musician what he thinks about critics is like asking a lamppost how it feels about dogs."[6]

Music is an undeniably powerful force. Throughout culture and society we can see its influence for both good and bad. We've seen the negative effects of music and the excesses of "sex, drugs and rock 'n roll." We need to be aware that music can harm. It informs our ideals and beliefs and can ultimately manipulate our attitudes and behavior. We are in danger of undoing any good work of the Spirit in us if we're constantly listening to music that encourages violence, misogyny, greed or other destructive values.

The Week magazine recently reported a somewhat less sinister reaction to listening to a particular type of music, a condition known as "glam rock shoulder!" It's a condition caused when partygoers punch the air in time to their favorite songs. Dr. George Rae said older people who aren't used to letting their hair down on the dance floor are most at risk of suffering from "glam rock shoulder."[7] You have been warned!

While we need to be wise about the music we listen to, I wonder whether at times the Church has become afraid of music, fearful of it being used to manipulate and afraid of it becoming an idol. As a result, we've kept music at arm's length. Consequently, it has been the world that sets the standard for great-sounding music. All too often the Church has been a few years behind the pace, settling for imitation rather than trailblazing.

William Booth, founder of the Salvation Army, took songs that were being sung in pubs and on the streets and set godly lyrics to these well-loved melodies. It was Booth who coined the phrase, "Why should the devil have all the best tunes?"[8]

For his Christmas message to *War Cry* readers of 1880, William Booth wrote:

> Secular music, do you say, belongs to the devil? Does it? Well, if it did I would plunder him for it, for he has no right to a single note . . . Every note, and every strain, and every harmony is divine, and belongs to us . . . So consecrate your voice and your instruments. Bring out your comets and harps and organs and flutes and violins and pianos and drums, and everything else that can make melody. Offer them to God, and use them to make all the hearts about you merry before the Lord.[9]

I love the passion and purpose of Booth. As God's people in today's society, music is one of the greatest mediums we have to communicate and express the gospel message. We are in relationship with the Creator of the universe, the God who designed and breathed music into being—it should be His children who create heavenly sounds that mold and shape culture. We should be setting the trends. The world should be looking to the Church to discover great sounding melodies and songs.

*   *   *

In an interview in *Spin* magazine, Bono said, "I always believed that music is a transcendent thing, a healing thing."[10] Bono is not alone in his views. The great German reformer Martin Luther once said:

> Next to the Word of God, music deserves the highest praise. She is a mistress and governess of those human emotions which control men or more often overtake them. Whether you wish to comfort the sad, to subdue frivolity, to encourage the despairing, to humble the proud, to calm the passionate or to appease those full of hate . . . what more affective means than music could you find?[11]

It is a revolutionary notion: Our songs and sounds can "comfort the sad" and "encourage the despairing." These are the songs that I want to listen to. (Dare I say it? These are the songs I want to write.)

In 1 Samuel, we read an intriguing story about David, who was called to play music for King Saul:

> Now the Spirit of the LORD had departed from Saul, and an evil spirit from the LORD tormented him.
>
> Saul's attendants said to him, "See, an evil spirit from God is tormenting you. Let our lord command his servants here to search for someone who can play the harp. He will play when the evil spirit from God comes upon you, and you will feel better."
>
> So Saul said to his attendants, "Find someone who plays well and bring him to me."

One of the servants answered, "I have seen a son of Jesse of Bethlehem who knows how to play the harp. He is a brave man and a warrior. He speaks well and is a fine-looking man. And the LORD is with him."

Then Saul sent messengers to Jesse and said, "Send me your son David, who is with the sheep." So Jesse took a donkey loaded with bread, a skin of wine and a young goat and sent them with his son David to Saul.

David came to Saul and entered his service. Saul liked him very much, and David became one of his armor-bearers. Then Saul sent word to Jesse, saying, "Allow David to remain in my service, for I am pleased with him."

Whenever the spirit from God came upon Saul, David would take his harp and play. Then relief would come to Saul; he would feel better, and the evil spirit would leave him (16:14-23).

This remarkable story suggests that God can use music to release people from evil manifestations and bring healing and restoration. In a dark and dangerous situation, David allowed his beautiful melodies of worship to rise up, and as a result, relief and light broke in. Can you begin to imagine an army of well-accomplished musical worshipers, dedicated to crafting the very best music, heading out to the pubs and clubs to play music over a broken and hurting world, bringing their worship into the dark places? Dare we believe that God can use our songs to bring healing, hope and restoration?

*   *   *

There is a song that I would give anything to hear. I've heard faint whispers of it, a glimpse of a lyric here and there. It is the song of our Father singing over His beloved:

> The Lord Your God is with you. He is mighty to save. He will take great delight in you. He will quiet you with His love. He will rejoice over you with singing (Zeph. 3:14).

I find it is easy to comprehend the idea of music as a gift *for us* to use to respond to God's love, but I find it completely unfathomable that God rejoices over us *with singing*. I wonder what that song could possibly sound like—without question, a song like no other!

Another passage from C. S. Lewis's *The Magician's Nephew* sees Aslan continuing to sing life into being:

> The Lion was pacing to and fro about that empty land and singing his new song. It was softer and more lilting than the song by which he had called up the star and the sun; a gentle, rippling music. And as he walked and sang the valley grew green with grass. It spread out from the Lion like a pool. It ran up the sides of the little hills like a wave.[12]

The gentle song of the Father brings life and hope to all. Like the rippling effect of a pebble thrown into a pool, this song spreads out, knowing no limits or bounds.

One of our challenges as worshipers is to tune in to this song. Like tuning in a radio, we need to keep listening and waiting until this melody gets louder and clearer. I believe that it is here that we will find so much of our own personal healing and gather a greater sense of worth. Not only that, but it is here that we will gain a sense of the Father's heart for the prodigals. One of my dreams is to see musicians tune in to the Father's song and allow the melody to bring transformation. If we could learn to communicate and express this sound through our guitars, drums, cellos, keyboards, voices or whatever we play, I truly believe we will see many people saved.

What do these songs sound like? They are raw, authentic, passionate, heartfelt, costly, daring and extravagant: divine, Spirit-breathed moments of creativity that reach out impacting the lives of many. I think of a friend of mine, who doesn't yet know Jesus, but tells me of the immense peace she finds every time she listens to a worship CD I gave her. I think of the letter I received from the parents of a girl who breathed her last breath, full of hope, listening to a simple song of worship. I think of different friends of mine, venturing into dingy clubs throughout the country to play their music, offering a message of love and redemption.

I love the scene in the film *The Color Purple* in which a crowd of "unchurched" people start flooding in to the church as they are led by the powerful sound of the choir worshiping with all their hearts. I remember crying as I watched, longing for the day when we would see people overwhelmed by the beauty and wonder of God, drawn to the Father by the sounds the Church was making. The moment we realize that the Glorious One whispers our names and sweetly sings over us, we will sing a sweeter song.

In Greek mythology, the seductive allure of the Sirens was infamous. Sailors were mysteriously lured to shore by the irresistible sound of their songs. Distracted by what they were hearing, the sailors failed to notice the hidden rocks below the surface of the sea, and as their boats began to sink the Sirens set to work devouring and consuming their flesh.

The story goes that one day Jason, another infamous character in ancient mythology, was set to sail past the island of the Sirens. Aware of the danger, he ordered the most talented musician, Orpheus, to play the most beautiful and melodious songs as they passed by. Jason and his men were so captivated by the music Orpheus played that no one on the boat was distracted by the dangerous sound of the Sirens. Instead, they heard a sweeter song.

We are surrounded by music. It is all around us as we shop, eat, walk, work, relax—we can't escape it. Like the songs of the Sirens, so many sounds lead people astray with lyrics and messages that are divisive and destructive. But as the hymn states, "Hark! How the heavenly anthem drowns all music but its own."[13] The sound of heaven, the song of redemption and the shout of salvation will one day drown out all other music. Even now, we have an opportunity to sing this most glorious song here on Earth.

Might we believe that we could write songs that transform people's lives? Our responsibility is to give of ourselves to become the best musicians we can be—not so that we can look amazing, but rather so that the world can better hear the song of heaven. When we start thinking like this, it changes everything. Every time we practice, every hour we rehearse, every moment we labor over lyrics, our hearts are pleading, "God, glorify Your name. Use us to express Your heart and to communicate the sound of heaven." Making music becomes so much more than music and songs—it becomes the sound of the kingdom of God coming on the earth.

*   *   *

Music should excite us. It is a God-given gift to be enjoyed. In the book of Revelation, a sign of God's punishment in the fall of Babylon is that "the music of harpists and musicians, flute players and trumpeters will never be heard in you again" (Rev. 18:22). God created music and everyday He sings it over us. As we've seen, creation is exploding in song.

We have a choice, though: to worship music or to worship God. If we want to hear "God songs" played on the radio and listened to in the clubs, our highest priority must be God. Before we look to the music, we must look to Him. We can't create these songs in our own strength—it is a spiritual activity. We want people to be left with the fragrance of Jesus. We want their hearts to be tugged by the Holy Spirit. We want their lives to be overwhelmed by the love of the Father.

There was a tremendous celebration when Solomon completed the Temple and the Ark of the Covenant was set in place. All the priests and musicians were gathered for this historic occasion:

> All the Levites who were musicians—Asaph, Heman, Jeduthun and their sons and relatives—stood on the east side of the altar, dressed in fine linen and playing cymbals, harps and lyres. They were accompanied by 120 priests sounding trumpets. The trumpeters and singers joined in unison, as with one voice, to give praise and thanks to the LORD. Accompanied by trumpets, cymbals and other instruments, they raised their voices in praise to the LORD and sang, "He is good; his love endures forever." Then the temple of the LORD was filled with a cloud, and the priests could not perform their service because of the cloud, for the glory of the LORD filled the temple of God (2 Chron. 5:12-14).

The Levites playing cymbals, harps and lyres, 120 priests on trumpets and the singers joining in with one voice—what a sound! But I wonder what it was that, over time, people remembered from that day? As impressive as that sound must have been, I speculate that their lasting memory was their extraordinary encounter with God as the Temple was filled majestically with His glory.

It is the God behind the music that we must seek. Let us love music and embrace the glorious gift that it is, let us join with creation, praising God in song, let us tune in to the sound of heaven in the hope that our music might lead others to God. But above all, let us pursue the giver of music, the God who rejoices over us with singing.

> Come Thou fount of every blessing,
> tune my heart to sing Your praise.[14]

I Am Yours, Jesus, You Are Mine

In June 2005, my wife, Rachel, and I headed off to the country of Tanzania to spend a week visiting some development projects with the charity Tearfund. We weren't sure what to expect, but we instantly loved it. The warmth of the people, the beauty of the surroundings and the buzz of activity all around us got under our skin. It was, however, a bittersweet experience. Through the smiles, singing and dancing was death, disease, sorrow, injustice, poverty and extreme hunger. One moment we were laughing, the next we were at a total loss for words.

On our visit we had the opportunity to meet some incredible people. One lady whose smile will stay with us forever was Joyce Mbwilo. Living in a village called Uhambingeto, Joyce told us her story of life and survival. With no clean accessible water in the village, she would leave each night at midnight with an empty container, walk for over 10 hours and return home at 10 A.M. the following day with water for her family, totally exhausted.

It has been estimated that Joyce has walked the equivalent of three times around the earth in the pursuit of water. Thankfully, through Tearfund's work with local churches, significant steps are being made to improve life for the people in that village and many others like it, and put right the injustice they have suffered.

But how could that situation of profound inequity still be possible in a world today where so many of us have so much? When it comes to survival, I "want" for nothing. Water is accessible at the turn of a tap. I have food in the fridge and a car in the driveway. There are few things in life that I find myself urgently pursuing. I was deeply struck by the courage and steely determination of Joyce. Lying down and giving up was never an option. Driven by love for her family and an acute awareness of the necessity of clean water for survival, Joyce went to extreme measures to keep her family alive.

O God, You are my God, earnestly I seek You; my soul thirsts for You, my body longs for You, in a dry and weary land where there is no water . . . Because Your love is better than life, my lips will glorify You (Ps. 63:1,3).

My soul yearns, even faints, for the courts of the Lord; my heart and my flesh cry out for the living God (Ps. 84:2).

These verses from the psalms express an aching and longing that is often sadly lacking in my life. The object of King David's desire was God. More than life, more than anything else the world could ever offer, David wanted to see and know Him. In Jesus, we find living water that will satisfy our deepest thirst. This alone should inspire us to pursue more of Him, no matter the cost, no matter how long it takes or how far we have to go to get there. We need to chase after God. As Joyce walked through the night for decades to find water, are we willing to give all we have in order to discover something more important than even water: life itself?

*   *   *

Without doubt, the happiest day of my life was when I married the woman of my dreams. All my favorite people gathered together to celebrate our marriage—it was a perfect day. Since then, Rachel and I have learned what it means to live together and share life. It's been quite a steep learning curve! I have two younger brothers and grew up in a very "male" house, and as a result, women have always been something of a mystery to me. Over recent years, I have learned many things about the mystery of the female psyche, but one key discovery (and this is a generalization, but generalizations are generally true!) is that women need to be cherished. They need to be wooed, romanced and adored.

Sometimes Rachel will say to me, "Tim, you haven't said how beautiful I am today."

To this I want to reply, "Rachel, I told you how beautiful you were last week! Can't we have an agreement that unless I say otherwise, you should assume that I think you are beautiful?" (Marriage counselors—fear not! I don't actually say it!)

Perhaps my biggest mistake in our relationship was when we were dating. We had reached the stage of our relationship where we were beginning to talk about marriage. One afternoon we were talking together and Rachel shared how much she loved me and said that she knew beyond a shadow of a doubt that I was the one for her. I wanted to say something equally romantic back to her in response, but all I could hear coming out of my mouth was, "Rachel, I'm 99 percent sure as well." Apparently 99 percent isn't good enough!

If I want to have a healthy relationship with my wife, I need to take time to be intimate with her and to express my love for her. If I don't, then pretty soon our relationship will turn sour. It is the same with God: If we are not drawing close to Him and seeking His face, our relationship suffers. To keep the flame alive, we need to keep making an effort to adore Him. So simple, yet sadly too often we get distracted. We are too busy, overworked, stressed and overwhelmed, and we don't take time out to be still and know that He is God.

G. K. Chesterton once wrote, "Sometimes our religion is more a theory than a love affair." We need to find time to be intimate with our Savior, to respond to His mercy and enjoy Him forever. We were made for intimacy, to know and to be known. When deprived of intimacy, we suffer. There is a vacuum within us that craves to be loved and accepted for who we are.

In 1996, the U.S. Masters golf championship, one of the most prestigious of golfing prizes, took place. A lot was at stake. On the final day, Greg Norman and Nick Faldo went head to head. With a six shot lead, the championship appeared to have Norman's name written all over it, but all did not go according to plan. In only a short amount of time, the tables had turned—by the eighteenth green, an ashen-faced Norman watched Nick Faldo sink a putt that won him the coveted Green Jacket and crowned him the U.S. Masters champion.

In a sporting gesture, Faldo embraced Norman, and to the great shock of millions of viewers Norman broke down in tears. Afterward at the press conference, Greg Norman was pressed to explain the reason for his breakdown. He told them that as a child his father had not shown him any warmth or affection and would only ever shake his hand. When Nick Faldo hugged him, he realized that it was the first time he had been hugged as a grown man. In that moment, something inside of him broke.

*   *   *

We live in a society that drives us toward success. We all know a sense of pressure to succeed and make something of our lives. Our culture places pressure on us to get high exam results, to get into the right university, to get a great job, to earn lots of money, to get married, to have the perfect family, to own a home and to make our lives count for something. At every stage in life, there is pressure to succeed. Pressure, pressure, pressure.

And this pressure to be successful can drive us into the ground.

Recently the *Daily Telegraph* ran an article entitled "How the Pressure to Succeed Is Creating a Generation of Unruly, Depressed Teenagers." The article stated that the number of 15-year-olds suffering from anxiety and depression has increased by 70 percent since the mid-1980s.[1] Even worse, we are seeing the rate of teenage suicide grow as the years go by. I was devastated to hear of an old school friend of mine who committed suicide at university. I remember how stressed he would get when exam time came around. His parents were desperate for him to succeed and he was anxious to live up to their expectations, but at university his studies did not go as well as he had hoped. Having failed his exams, he concealed the truth from his parents, dreading their disappointment, and after months of deception it all became too much. What a tragic waste of a life.

Success is not only measured by our achievements. Success is about our need to be accepted, our need to be loved. Driven by this need, we push ourselves to try to earn respect and gain acceptance. We work crazy hours to achieve promotion. We push our bodies to the limits to make the grade. But is it ever enough? As Freddie Mercury, the lead singer of Queen, said:

> You can have everything in the world and still be the loneliest man, and that is the most bitter type of loneliness. Success has brought me world idolization and millions of pounds, but it's prevented me from having the one true thing we all need—a loving, ongoing relationship.[2]

I recognize in my own life a need for acceptance and significance. I frequently feel the pressure to succeed as a husband, as a worship leader, as a songwriter, as a friend, even as a Christian. The desire to be loved is not a purely misguided perception, and my hopes and dreams are not wrong in themselves. But sometimes my desire for success becomes an unhealthy distraction, a warped sense of trying to continually earn something that is beyond me. It leaves me exhausted and frustrated. *If only I could write that song. If only I could achieve that goal.*

The wonderful truth about our God is that He loves us more than we could ever begin to comprehend. Recently a friend shared this phrase with me and it has stuck in my head, challenging, inspiring and reforming me: "I am loved by God and I love God—therefore I am successful." Allow these words to sink into your heart. Perhaps this is the antidote to society's pressure to achieve? Could this simple truth be the real secret of success?

Regardless of who we are and what we have done, God has made it plain that He unconditionally loves us. No achievement in life could ever top

that—there is nothing in this world that could bring us greater happiness or fulfillment. It all starts with us receiving God's unfailing, initiated love. Like Michelangelo's painting in the Sistine Chapel, God reaches down to touch each one of us. "We love because He first loved us" (1 John 4:19). We may be programmed to try to earn love, but God makes it clear that first and foremost we must receive His love. It is a gift to us freely given.

When my nephew Noah was born, I went to visit him and his parents in the hospital. There, he was sleeping away, totally oblivious to the pain and stress he had caused his mum and dad—particularly his mum! The labor had lasted over 36 hours, and that was just the beginning: Noah needed to be fed three or four times a night, so his parents were exhausted. And if all that wasn't enough, Noah's needs had cost a small fortune: strollers, diapers, clothes, toys, car seats, a newly decorated nursery. With Noah it was one-way traffic. Take, take, take. There was no "thanks Mum and Dad for bringing me into this world." Not even a smile to say thank you. How ungrateful! But looking at his mum and dad, you could see that they totally adored him. They loved him with all their hearts—in a moment, he had become their pride and joy. Noah did not earn his parents love. They loved him because he was theirs.

We could learn a lesson or two from Noah.

If we look at Jesus' ministry in the book of Matthew, we see this amazing moment when He is baptized by His cousin John. As soon as Jesus came out of the water, the heavens opened and a voice declared, "This is my Son, whom I love; with him I am well pleased" (Matt. 3:17). Before Jesus had performed any great miracles, before He had healed anyone, before He had raised anyone from the dead—His father was pleased with Him.

If we want to be a people that impact this world, there is something crucial we must learn: We must learn to be loved by God. We need to learn to accept the free gift of God's love, that it cannot be earned, that it is not distributed according to our success. We need to embrace Him and learn to enjoy all that He has showered upon us. As this truth becomes the rock on which we build our lives, then we can boldly step out, knowing that if God is for us, who can be against us (see Rom. 8:31)?

In King David we see this assured boldness. For all his mistakes and failures (of which there were many), he had an unshakable understanding of God's unceasing love for him. Reading through some of the psalms, his confidence is quite startling.

In Psalm 17:8, David prays, "Keep me as the apple of Your eye." (Refreshing that David assumes that he's *already* the apple of God's eye!)

In Psalm 18:19 he declares, "He brought me out into a spacious place; he rescued me because He delighted in me." Such boldness and confidence in God's heart of love.

In Psalm 41:11, David says to God, "I know that you are pleased with me." How many of us could say that with confidence before our God?

In Psalm 139:13-16, he pens these famous words:

> For You created my inmost being;
> you knit me together in my mother's womb.
> I praise you because I am fearfully and wonderfully made;
> your works are wonderful,
> I know that full well.
> My frame was not hidden from you
> when I was made in the secret place.
> When I was woven together in the depths of the earth,
> your eyes saw my unformed body.

These verses suggest that David did not link his earthly success—or lack of it—with his acceptance of God's love. We too need to journey toward the realization that God's love for us is constant, despite the things we do or don't do. It is imperative that we grasp what David knew to be true: We are loved and adored. No arrogance, just truth. David lived in the certainty that he was loved by God. For David, this was the pinnacle of success. In moments of sinfulness, he stood before God and said, "Here I am, God. I've messed up again, but *I know You love me.*" When he was full of doubt and fear, he could say, "God, where are You? Why have You deserted me? Don't let me go, because *I know You love me.*" Free and abandoned before his King, with childlike faith, David boldly approached God's throne and courageously lived out his beliefs. He was a passionate and extravagant worshiper who found meaning and contentment in the eyes of his Father.

I remember on a particular occasion being profoundly challenged by God's love for me. A top London banker, who happened to be a Christian, called me one day and invited me for lunch. As we ate, he hesitantly mentioned that he felt he had an encouragement for me. He felt God had given him a picture of me kneeling down before the Lord, singing to Him these words from the song "Here I Am to Worship":

> You're altogether lovely,
> Altogether worthy,
> Altogether wonderful to me.[3]

Then he saw the Lord sing those same words over me. Initially, I found that picture really hard to accept—surely God couldn't sing that over me! But the stunning truth is that God does indeed delight in us and rejoice over us with singing. I left that lunch meeting overcome with the depth of God's love for me.

*   *   *

So how do we respond to this love? By giving all that we are in response.

The former vicar of Holy Trinity Brompton, Bishop Sandy Millar, tells the story of attending a church conference. Having been dramatically inspired by all that was going on, he went for a walk along the beach to pour out his heart to God. He was so thankful for all that was going on in the life of Holy Trinity. As he prayed, he was suggesting things that he could offer up for God to use. When he asked the question, *God, what do You want from me?* He felt God clearly say, "Sandy, all I want is you." Before we get caught up making grand statements and trying to offer God our money, achievements and ambitions, we need to first and foremost offer up ourselves—all that we are, all that we have been and all that we will ever be.

Living for Your Glory

CHAPTER 7

LIVING FOR YOUR GLORY

How great is our God? The universe we live in is vast. As we look up and consider the enormity of our God, we get perspective. We learn to embrace the smallness of who we are.

Daily our senses are bombarded with a message that we are the most important thing on the face of the earth.

"Buy this, you're worth it."

"Treat yourself, you deserve it."

Recently I read a story about a business tycoon dubbed "Britain's vainest man." He had spent about $108,000 on a new set of teeth and twice daily injected himself with growth hormones at an annual cost of almost $20,000. He dedicated one wall of his penthouse to a $20,000 portrait of himself. And if that wasn't enough, the 31-year-old has spent almost $6 million on an entire Bulgarian coastal town, which he renamed after himself.[1]

We are led to believe that the world revolves around us. As one ad slogan says, "It's all about you." A brief flick through the Scriptures or a walk through spectacular scenery, however, quickly raises the question, Is there something bigger or greater than us? The world *does* revolve around Someone, but it isn't you and it certainly isn't me. Whose name are we living for? Are we living to make God famous or to make ourselves famous?

*   *   *

From generation to generation, the story of David and Goliath has been told and retold with relish and excitement. On one hill the Philistine army assembled, prepared and ready for war. On another hill, under Saul's command, the Israelite army gathered. Twice a day, the towering figure of the Philistine warrior Goliath screamed and shouted threats and abuse to the Israelite army. The gauntlet had been laid: Send a man from the Israelite ranks to fight Goliath. If he overcame and killed the nine-foot giant, the Philistines would become subject to the Israelites. If Goliath was victorious, however, it was game over for Israel. For 40 days, every morning and every evening, Goliath took his stand, terrifying and dismaying the Israelite army.

Among the most fearsome and trained warriors of Israel, not one was willing to take on his challenge. That is, until David son of Jesse, a young shepherd boy, overheard Goliath's fearsome rant. David, angered by Goliath's torrent of abuse and appalled that he should defy the army of the living God, boldly declared, "Let no one lose heart on account of this Philistine; your servant will go and fight him" (1 Sam. 17:32). There must have been a ripple of laughter among the Israelite army. What chance would David have? It was absurd.

We know the story. David, after persuading King Saul, stepped out armed with a sling and five smooth stones. With one shot, a single stone crashed into Goliath's forehead, knocking him dead. David had conquered. He was victorious. Against the odds, Israel had a new hero.

Notice something: At no point before stepping out to fight did David mention his own name. Twice when speaking to King Saul, he referred to himself simply as "your servant":

Your servant will go and fight him (1 Sam. 17:32).

Your servant has been keeping his fathers sheep (1 Sam. 17:34).

Only after David had slain Goliath did Saul turn to the commander of the army and ask, "'Abner, whose son is that man?' Abner replied, 'As surely as you live, O king, I don't know'" (1 Sam. 17:55).

LIVING FOR YOUR GLORY

How great is our God? The universe we live in is vast. As we look up and consider the enormity of our God, we get perspective. We learn to embrace the smallness of who we are.

David had achieved the unthinkable and no one had a clue who he was. If I had been in David's shoes, I would have made sure *everyone* knew my name. I would have played the martyr card: "My name is Tim Hughes. If I die heroically and people want to honor me by building a statue, please take my correct measurements. I'm six-feet tall. If possible, could you add a six pack?" I would have wanted to go out in a blaze of glory. Not so for David. He was not bothered about his own press. He was focused and determined on directing all eyes to the God he so passionately loved and worshiped.

In the film *Amadeus*, the life story of Wolfgang Amadeus Mozart is told through the eyes of fellow composer Antonio Salieri. As court composer to Emperor Joseph II, Salieri was also a highly gifted composer, but he was wracked with jealousy and bitterness, living his life despising the astonishing natural gift and skill of Mozart. There is a telling scene in which a young Salieri, alone in church, prays to God:

> Lord, make me a great composer! Let me celebrate your glory through music—and be celebrated myself. Make me famous throughout the world, dear God. Make me immortal![2]

How often in the quietness of our hearts do we recite a similar prayer? There are sentiments in Salieri's prayer that are honorable and upright, aspects that we would do well to pray ourselves. "Lord, make me a great composer!" In all that we do, we need to pray for God's inspiration to enable us to be the best that we can be. This is not in itself a selfish prayer. The prayer continues, "Let me celebrate your glory through music . . ." We must seek to celebrate God's glory through whatever we do, be it teaching, art, film, law, medicine, design, *whatever*. What a wonderful prayer—that God's glory

How great is our God? The universe we live in is vast. As we look up and consider the enormity of our God, we get perspective. We learn to embrace the smallness of who we are.

would be demonstrated and enjoyed as we excel in our God-given gifts.

But it's here that the prayer turns inward and sour: ". . . and be celebrated myself. Make me famous throughout the world, dear God. Make me immortal!" For Salieri (and for us), this is the catch. The real desire of his heart was that he would be recognized and adored.

I sometimes find myself praying a similar prayer: "God, I want these songs to bring glory and fame to You, but please may I become successful through it as well." Or the even more subtle and insidious request, dressed up in spiritual language: "Lord, allow me to minister on a bigger platform so that many more people will come to know and worship You." It almost sounds honorable—surely it is a good thing that many come to know and love God! But so often that is not my highest aim. Like Salieri, I crave people's praise, and this prayer reveals the pride and arrogance that darkens my heart. Am I passionate about God's renown or my own? Would I be equally passionate about leading worship and writing songs if I only ever led before a small group of people?

There is a verse that appears twice in Luke's Gospel: "For everyone who exalts himself will be humbled, and he who humbles himself with be exalted" (Luke 14:11; 18:14). It is interesting to note that this verse is based around active verbs. I used to think that humility was a gift that floated down from heaven to our laps—a person was either full of humility or full of pride. It was a personality trait that people were born with. Now my understanding has completely shifted. There is a responsibility for us to seek after humility, actively choosing to humble ourselves before a glorious God.

I still have the Bible I studied in my teenage years. Inscribed on the opening page is a heart-cry that I continue to pray: "I want to be a humble, passionate servant." If we don't passionately endeavor to pursue humility, to live for God's name, then we start living for our own names.

We start exalting ourselves. Every day we must actively chase after humility.

A while back, after one Sunday evening service, I was chatting to my keyboardist. A visitor to our church came up and asked me if I remembered the fourth or fifth song we had sung that night. I started going through song titles.

"Was it 'Open the Eyes of My Heart, Lord?'"

"No."

"What about 'Give Thanks to the Lord.'"

"No."

And then it dawned on me: *She means "Here I Am to Worship."*

Expecting her to share how she had been profoundly impacted by my little song, I gently sang the chorus to trigger her memory: "Here I am to worship, here I am to bow down, here I am to say that you're my God."

I stood back, waiting to have my ego stroked and she replied, "Oh, no! I hate that song. People at my church sing that song and whenever I hear it I want to vomit!"

Those were her exact words. My keyboardist was laughing so hard, he fell to the floor. I quickly steered the conversation away from the topic, hoping she wouldn't discover that I had written the tune, but in that moment, God reminded me that "whoever exalts himself will be humbled, and whoever humbles himself will be exalted" (Matt. 23:12). I had gotten carried away. I had started to think I was something special. Through that lady's words, God graciously reminded me that I'm just a guy who writes songs that make people want to vomit.

The Bible is clear: If we don't *choose* to bow down reverently before God, we will be humbled. He is God. We are not. He seems to prefer it that way. God's Word through the prophet Isaiah is a powerful reminder to us:

How great is our God? The universe we live in is vast. As we look up and consider the enormity of our God, we get perspective. We learn to embrace the smallness of who we are,

The LORD Almighty has a day in store for all the proud and lofty, for all that is exalted (and they will be humbled) . . . The arrogance of man will be brought low and the pride of men humbled; the LORD alone will be exalted in that day, and idols will totally disappear . . . In that day men will throw away to the rodents and bats their idols of silver and idols of gold, which they make to worship. They will flee to caverns in the rocks and to overhanging crags from dread of the LORD and the splendor of his majesty, when he rises to shake the earth. Stop trusting in man, who has but a breath in his nostrils. Of what account is he? (Isa. 2:12,17-18,20-22).

So how can we actively cultivate a heart of humility?

*   *   *

On August 20, 1977, Voyager II, the inter-planetary probe launched to observe and transmit back to Earth data about our galaxy, set off traveling faster than the speed of a bullet. On August 28, 1989, it reached planet Neptune, 2,700 million miles from Earth. Voyager II then left our solar system. It will not come within one light year of any star for 958,000 years. In our galaxy, there are 100,000 million stars like our sun. Our galaxy is one of 100,000 million galaxies.

In a throw away line in Genesis, the writer tells us, "He also made the stars." Read the last paragraph again, and then mull that statement over. How great is our God? The universe we live in is vast. As we look up and consider the enormity of our God, we get perspective. We learn to embrace the smallness of who we are.

Psalm 8 puts it beautifully:

> O LORD, our Lord, how majestic is your name in all the earth!
> You have set your glory above the heavens.
> From the lips of children and infants you have ordained praise
> because of your enemies, to silence the foe and the avenger.
> When I consider your heavens, the work of your fingers,
> the moon and the stars, which you have set in place,
> what is man that you are mindful of him,
> the son of man that you care for him?
> (vv. 1-4).

We are but a breath in comparison to Almighty God. The more we ponder and dwell on the glory of God, the more we can find perspective as to who we are.

*   *   *

A key way to cultivate a humble heart is to learn the art of servanthood. I love to serve. When there are lots of onlookers, I am amazing at doing the washing up or setting out chairs. Take the crowd away, however, and I'm reluctant to do any of those behind-the-scenes chores.

I was struck by the story of a well-known American worship leader. Feeling a call by God to lead worship, he approached his pastor to tell him of his availability to lead the worship at church. His pastor graciously informed him that there was no position available at the moment for a worship leader, but that they were looking for a janitor. Thinking this would be a short-term post before stepping up to become the worship leader, this guy took on the job. For weeks and then months, this man spent his days stacking chairs, cleaning toilets and locking up last thing at night.

As time went on, he became more and more bitter and frustrated. Why was he wasting his time on menial tasks that anyone could do? But one morning while mopping the floor, he suddenly had a revelation that what he was doing was worship. Every chair stacked, every light bulb repaired, every kind deed done to help others—if done to the glory of God—was a precious offering of worship. It was here that he learned the heart of worship.

God is looking for servants, not stars. In what ways are you choosing to serve those around you? How are you investing in obscurity by doing those jobs that no one sees and can give you credit for? As we invest in obscurity, I have no doubt that we will grow in humility.

*   *   *

Jealousy is an ugly trait. It is so sad to see people consumed by jealousy and resentment. At times it can be really hard to see our friends thrive and prosper when it feels like we are not. By putting others first and by choosing to rejoice in others' successes, we are choosing to humble ourselves.

Recently I was involved in a worship conference that was held in Australia. Throughout the week, most of the worship was wonderfully led by Darlene Zschech, writer of "Shout to the Lord." One afternoon I was down to lead with two other worship leaders from her team. We ran through a few songs and were prepared, but 10 minutes before the meeting, Darlene turned up. The two guys went straight up to her and said, "Darlene, you lead. It's so great when you lead it. We'll back you up."

LIVING FOR YOUR GLORY

How great is our God? The universe we live in is vast. As we look up and consider the enormity of our God, we get perspective. We learn to embrace the smallness of who we are.

She replied, "No, no—you guys lead. It will be so amazing if you lead it."

I stood back watching as they argued amongst themselves, each trying to persuade the other to lead. I wanted to step in and say, "Guys, I'll lead!"

What a model of a team preferring one another. There was such a strong sense of community and life in that place. There were no egos. It was a group of people passionate about drawing all the attention to God. I have no doubt that the humility of those involved has been formed and shaped by their desire to prefer one another. If you often find yourself thinking, *I should be leading there*, *I'm more gifted than her*, or *I write better songs than him*, choose to prefer others. Bless those you struggle with. Talk highly of those you feel envious of. Doing so will lead to humility.

In the eighteenth century, two theologians, George Whitfield and John Wesley, were well-documented as having strong and differing theological opinions. One day someone asked Whitfield the question, "Do you think we will see Mr. Wesley in heaven?"

"No, I don't think so," Whitfield responded.

As the crowd gasped in shock, he continued, "He will be so near the throne and we will be at the back of the crowd."

This is exactly the attitude we need to develop. We might not agree with everyone or even connect with all people, but wouldn't it be amazing if we could learn to prefer one another? Can you begin to imagine the impact of a Church united and choosing to honor and support one another?

When Ronald Regan was president of the United States, he had a sign on his desk saying, "There is no limit to how far a person can go as long as he doesn't care who gets the credit." We can get so preoccupied about who gets praised and credited for this and that, and before long, an unhealthy competitive streak rises to the surface. Let us remind ourselves of the big picture. To the church in Corinth—which was falling into the temptation of obsessing over prominent names and ministries—Paul wrote:

> What, after all is Apollos? And what is Paul? Only servants, through whom you came to believe . . . I planted the seed, Apollos watered it, but God made it grow. So neither he who plants nor he who waters is anything, but only God, who makes things grow (1 Cor. 3:5-7).

We need to hear and receive these words today. As we learn to prefer one another, we inwardly cultivate a humble heart. No longer are we consumed with our own personal gain. Rather, we long to see God's kingdom coming and His name lifted high above all other names—even our own.

LIVING FOR YOUR GLORY

How great is our God? The universe we live in is vast. As we look up and consider the enormity of our God, we get perspective. We learn to embrace the smallness of who we are.

Christ in Me, the Hope of Glory

A few years ago I met a retired Anglican bishop from South Africa. As we talked, he told me about his retirement plans. He had been unsure for months as to what the future would hold, but he kept on praying, "Lord, show me what I can do that You will bless."

For months he prayed that prayer, but felt God was silent. After a while, he realized that he'd been praying the wrong prayer the whole time. He felt God tell him what he needed to pray: "Lord, what is it that You are doing that I can bless?"

Our journey as worshipers should always be to find out what pleases the Lord (see Eph. 5:10), to find out what God is blessing and to get involved with that. Rather than a me-centered faith, we need to pursue a Him-centered faith. At the heart of worship, we as God's creation choose to center ourselves around Him, our Creator. We live to bless Him.

When I read the Bible, one thing seems abundantly clear: God is passionate about the poor. Jesus made that so apparent. "The Spirit of the Lord is on me, because He has anointed me to preach good news to the poor" (Luke 4:18). In Amos 5, God's heart burns with anger as He rebukes a people who offer up songs of worship and other choice offerings, but who trample and deprive the poor for their own selfish gain. We can't escape the truth that God's heart breaks for the last, the least and the lost. If I want to glorify God in all that I do, issues of justice and the poor need to be at the core of who I am.

Speaking at the U.S. National Prayer Breakfast in 2006, Bono remarked on God's heart for the poor:

> God is in the slums, in the cardboard boxes where the poor play house . . . God is in the silence of a mother who has infected her child with a virus that will end both their lives . . . God is in the cries heard under the rubble of war . . . God is in the debris of wasted opportunity and lives, and God is with us if we are with them [the poor].[1]

For my job, I get to travel all over the world leading worship at different churches and conferences. I get to work with some amazing people, hear inspiring speakers and see God move in remarkable ways. Recently I went on a ministry trip to South Africa with some friends from Soul Survivor. Compared to most trips, this one was fairly low-key. We led at a couple of

visiting different townships and projects throughout Durban. We spent one afternoon playing football with AIDS orphans. We spent a morning serving breakfast to homeless men. We spent time with a group of children who had learned to survive on the streets. We visited people's homes, we chatted, and at times we laughed and cried together. During the week, my heart was so stirred. I felt devastated at the injustice, and (strangely) fell more in love with Jesus. In the lives of the people I met, I encountered Christ. I can honestly say it was one of the best trips I have ever taken. There were no big meetings. We didn't see hundreds of lives changed. On the contrary—it was *our* lives that were radically changed.

As we worship, we change. Beholding is becoming. The more we look to Jesus and spend time adoring Him and unpack the Scriptures to ponder His character and nature, the more we will share His heart and obey His commands. Genuine worship will not only lead to our lives, but also our society, being transformed.

> Just as worship begins in holy expectancy, it ends with holy obedience. If worship does not propel us into greater obedience, it has not been worship.[2]

I love the story of Zacchaeus the tax collector. Intrigued to see who Jesus was, he climbed up a tree to see what all the fuss was about. Jesus looked past the crowd and into the tree where Zacchaeus sat, and said, "Zacchaeus, come down immediately. I must stay at your house today." Zacchaeus was overcome with joy and gladly welcomed Jesus into his home.

It's fascinating to read what he did next: Zacchaeus stood up and said to the Lord, "Look, Lord! Here and now I will give half my possessions to the poor, and if I have cheated anybody out of anything, I will pay back four times the amount" (Luke 19:8). We don't read that Jesus told Zacchaeus to do this—it was an impromptu, heartfelt response. Zacchaeus encountered Jesus and fell in love. His response was to give to the poor, to act justly.

Worship is the total alignment of our heart, soul, mind and strength with the will of God. When we worship, we will find we are led to the poor, and if we love Jesus, then we will gladly follow.

John Wesley, the great English evangelist, faced persecution and trials on many occasions. As he traveled and preached the word of God, he was often beaten, mocked and set upon by angry mobs. He faced malicious attacks on his personal character and beliefs. He suffered hardship and pain, yet in the midst of this adversity, he witnessed God do remarkable things. One time he was asked, "What is your secret?"

To this he replied, "Each morning I wake up and I set myself on fire for God. Then I go out and people watch me burn!"

Can you begin to imagine the impact we could have as God's people if every morning we looked to God and allowed the fullness of who He is to burn deeply within us for all the world to see? Sadly, as we've seen, we often look instead to ourselves and live lives relying on our own strength. But as my friend Louie Giglio says, "Attempting to orchestrate the world around us, even for a day, leaves us stressed and spent."[3]

Trying to light our own fire is futile. Seeking with every fiber of our being to shine in the darkness is pointless. We just can't do it. We are not meant to—our job is to reflect. Like a mirror reflecting an image, we are called to behold and reflect the glory of God. We are made in God's image, marked by Him. Wherever we go, whatever we do, we carry His likeness. Like John Wesley, our role is to burn with the fire that God enflames within us. We need to be consumed with Him. It is Christ in us, the hope of glory (see Col. 1:27).

There's a wonderful ease about it. The emphasis is not on us; it is on Him. Our job is to simply behold, enjoy and marvel. As we do, we are transformed. We embrace our smallness, and glory in God's vastness.

*   *   *

For many years I thought humility was about completely fading into nothing—becoming a nobody. The equation in my head was *Quiet person equals humble person, loud person equals arrogant person.* This could not be farther from the truth. Humility is about having a healthy perspective of who we are in relation to who God is. As John Eldridge says, "Shame says 'I'm nothing to look at. I'm not capable of goodness.' Humility says, 'I bear a glory for sure, but it's a reflected glory. A grace given to me.'"[4] Humility doesn't stop us from rising up. It doesn't keep us from living bold, brave, adventurous, passionate, strong, loud and exuberant lives. C. S. Lewis captured the sentiment of humility beautifully in his classic book *The Screwtape Letters,* which is cleverly written from the perspective of one demon to another, plotting to deceive and confuse Christians. One of the demons describes, with frustration, God's desire for humility in us:

> The Enemy [God] wants to bring a man to a state of mind in which he could design the best cathedral in the world and know it to be the best, and rejoice in the fact, without being any more (or less) or otherwise glad at having done it than he would be if it had been done by another. The Enemy wants him, in the end, to be so free from any bias in his own favour that he can rejoice in his own talents as frankly

or gratefully as in his neighbours talents—or in a sunrise, an elephant, or a waterfall. He wants each man, in the long run, to be able to recognise all creatures (even himself) as glorious and excellent things.[5]

What freedom we would feel if we could rejoice, when someone else excels, with the same wholehearted joy as displayed when we ourselves excel. Humility is not denying the talents God has given us—it is fully embracing every personal skill and success and thanking God for them, but with equal enthusiasm thanking God for the gifts and talents of those around us.

Now is not the time to shy away. These are days to rise up and reflect. Where are the doctors and scientists who will find a cure for AIDS? Where are the teachers who will educate and love a broken generation? Where are the songwriters who will write melodies of hope? Where are the politicians who will stand up for truth and justice? Where are those who will champion the stewardship of creation? Who among us will father the fatherless?

The stakes are high. We need to be a people who inwardly burn with passion and zeal for Christ—at all costs, at all times, and in all situations, determined worshipers in every season of the soul.

*   *   *

God is looking for a people that will honor and reflect His glory, come what may. I love the story of Shadrach, Meshach and Abednego in the fiery furnace. The Babylonian king, Nebuchadnezzar, set in place a new law. Erecting an image of gold, 99 feet high and 9 feet wide, the command was issued that when the sound of the horn, flute, zither, lyre, harp, pipes and other kinds

of music was heard, all must fall down and worship the golden image. Whoever refused would be immediately thrown into a blazing furnace to die. Shadrach, Meshach and Abednego made their stand and refused to bow the knee. Defiant before the king, they declared, "If we are thrown into the blazing furnace, the God we serve is able to save us from it, and he will rescue us from your hand, O king. But even if he does not, we want you to know, O king, that we will not serve your gods or worship the image of gold you have set up" (Dan. 3:17-18). Incensed with rage, Nebuchadnezzar ordered the furnace to be heated seven times hotter than usual. The furnace became so hot that even the men who threw Shadrach, Meshach and Abednego in were killed.

As Nebuchadnezzar sat down to watch the death of these three men, he saw a sight that startled him. Rising to his feet he asked his advisors, "Weren't there three that we tied up and threw into the fire? Look! I see four men walking around the fire, unbound and unharmed, and the fourth looks like a son of the gods" (Dan. 3:24-25). Approaching the furnace, Nebuchadnezzar called out, "Shadrach, Meshach and Abednego, servants of the Most High God, come out! Come here!"

To everyone's bewilderment, Shadrach, Meshach and Abednego walked out unharmed—there was not event the smell of burning on them. Stirred by this miracle, Nebuchadnezzar praised their God.

In the face of death, these three men chose to worship. At great cost to themselves, they chose to honor God. Remarkably, God intervened and rescued them from certain death, and as a result, His name was glorified.

Graham Staines, an Australian missionary, spent 34 years working among the lepers in India, educating the young and spreading the good news of the gospel. One day in January 1999, Graham and his two young sons were working among the poorest of the poor in a local village. With nowhere to sleep, they found shelter in their station wagon. During the night, Hindu extremists surrounded the van, chained the handles of the doors shut, set fire to the station wagon and fled.

Echoes of Shadrach, Meshach and Abednego. What would God do? Would He rescue them from the fiery furnace and glorify His name?

When the fire finally cooled, rescuers found the charred body of Graham Staines with his arms wrapped around the bodies of his sons. Left behind to mourn was Graham's wife and daughter, Gladys and Esther. The Indian media descended on Gladys's doorstep to capture her reaction. Her response was quoted in every newspaper across India, a nation of one billion people, the following morning:

> I have only one message for the people of India. I am not bitter, neither am I angry. But I have one great desire, that each citizen of this country should establish a personal relationship with Jesus Christ, who gave His life for their sins . . . let us burn hatred and spread the flame of Christ's love.[6]

In that moment, the gospel message was proclaimed throughout the nation. As Gladys chose to forgive, to honor God, to ultimately worship, God was glorified and a nation was profoundly impacted. John Piper writes, "God seldom calls us to an easier life, but always calls us to know more of him and drink more deeply of his sustaining grace."[7]

In every situation that comes our way, our role is to center our lives around Christ and allow Him to glorify His name in and through us. In every trial of life, every circumstance, through battles and blessings, it is Christ in me the hope of glory. We're not called to muster up superhuman strength. God doesn't leave us on our own to fight His corner. We're called to surrender our lives to Him, holding nothing back. He is the all-powerful God, mighty to act, the God who has the whole world in His hands. As we say yes to Him, following His ways no matter the cost, we will see God's transforming resurrection power.

Holding
Nothing Back

When Rick Hoyt was born in 1962, the umbilical chord coiled around his neck and cut off oxygen to his brain, leaving him a quadriplegic. His parents, Dick and Judy, were told that there was no hope for their child's development. Despite being told that Rick would be a vegetable all his life, his parents were determined to raise him as normally as possible. Being unable to speak, a group of engineers built Rick a specially designed interactive computer that allowed him to communicate his thoughts by using the slight head movements that he could manage.

At the age of 15, Rick told his father that he wanted to participate in a five-mile benefit run for a local lacrosse player who had been paralyzed in an accident. Out of love for his son, Dick, who had never previously done any long-distance running, agreed to push Rick in his wheelchair. They finished next-to-last, but were elated with their achievement. Overwhelmed by the experience, Rick managed to communicate to his parents that for the first time in his life, competing in that race, he didn't feel disabled. Spurred on by this revelation, father and son, "Team Hoyt," began entering more races.

After four years of marathons, they attempted their first triathlon—a combination of 26.2 miles of running, 112 miles of cycling and 2.4 miles of swimming. To date, they have raced in 64 marathons (with a personal best of 2:40:47), 78 half-marathons and 206 triathlons. And they once trekked 3,735 miles across America. Their achievements become all the more staggering when you consider that when Dick runs, he pushes Rick in his wheelchair. When Dick cycles, Rick is in a specially designed seat attached to the front of his bike. When Dick swims, he pulls Rick in a heavy, stabilized boat attached to his waist.

Watching film footage of Team Hoyt competing together is phenomenally moving. Driven by love for his son and a desire to see him fulfilled, Dick has gone to unimaginable lengths to make him feel alive. In every race, it is the father, Dick, who does all the work, giving every ounce of strength for the sake of his son. Rick cannot offer any physical support—in fact, he only makes more work for his father. But witness Dick's affirmation of his son and watch Rick's face as he crosses the finish line, and you might think that the son had won the race singlehandedly.[1]

The story of Dick and Rick Hoyt is a powerful reminder of our Father's love for and commitment to us—the Father, who gave everything that we might know life in all its fullness. Holding nothing back, the Father delights in us, sings over us, chases after us, cares deeply about us and sent His only Son to die for us.

What is our only possible response to this extravagant love? To hold nothing back in return.

Chapter Notes

Chapter 1

1. A. W. Tozer, *The Knowledge of the Holy* (New York: Harper Collins, 1961), p. vii.
2. Quoted in Raniero Cantalamessa, *Come Creator Spirit* (Collegeville, MN: Liturgical Press, 2003), p. 10.
3. Wayne Grudem, *Bible Doctrine* (Downers Grove, IL: InterVarsity Press, 1999), p. 72.
4. "Amazing Facts About the Human Body," Arizona Science Center, Phoenix, AZ. http://www.azscience.org/bw3/amazing_facts.php (accessed March 2007).
5. "Human Lung," Wikipedia.com. http://en.wikipedia.org/wiki/Human_lung (accessed March 2007).
6. Dr. Robert E. Wallace, ed., *The San Andreas Fault System, California* (Washington, D.C.: United States Government Printing Office, 1990). Online version available at http://www.johnmartin.com/earthquakes/eqsafs/safs_431.htm (accessed March 2007).
7. Grudem, *Bible Doctrine,* p. 75.
8. Bernard of Cluny, quoted from Tozer, *The Knowledge of the Holy*, p. 42.
9. Robert Webber, quoted in Paul Basden, *Exploring the Worship Spectrum* (Grand Rapids, MI: Zondervan, 2004), p. 179.
10. Tozer, *The Knowledge of the Holy*, p. 65.
11. S. M. Lockridge, "That's My King," sermon delivered in 1976 at Calvary Baptist Church, San Diego, California.

Chapter 2

1. To find out more about Alpha, visit www.alpha.org.
2. Tim Hughes, "Beautiful One," © 2002 Worshiptogether.com Music, Brentwood, TN.
3. Matt Redman, "The Heart of Worship," © 2000 Birdwing Music, Brentwood, TN.
4. John Piper, *Desiring God* (Sisters, OR: Multnomah, 2003).
5. John Stott, *Romans: God's Good News for the World* (Downers Grove, IL: InterVarsity Press, 1995).

Chapter 3

1. Saint Bonaventure of Bagnoregio, *The Journey of the Mind into God*, from the Catholic Forum. http://www.catholic-forum.com/saints/stb16012.htm (accessed March 2007).
2. "Scientists Watch as Neutron Star Explodes," *Red Orbit News,* February 24, 2007. http://www.redorbit.com/news/space/46559/scientists_watch_as_neutron_star_explodes/index.html (accessed March 2007).

3. "Nifty Astronomy Facts," AOL hometown. http://users.aol.com/usgoju/nifty.html (accessed April 2007).
4. Taken from "The Week," Health and Science section, issue 595, January 6, 2007.
5. Andrew Byatt, Alistair Fothergill and Martin Holmes, "The Blue Planet," BBC Worldwide Limited, 2001.
6. "Grand Canyon," Wikipedia.org. http://en.wikipedia.org/wiki/Grand_Canyon (accessed March 2007).
7. John Wesley Powell, *The Exploration of the Colorado River and Its Canyons* (New York: Penguin, 1987).
8. "Amazing Facts About Our Body," Sortlifeout.co.uk. http://www.meaningoflife.i12.com/body.htm (accessed April 2007). "Human Body," Useless Facts. http://facts.330.ca/body/ (accessed April 2007).
9. C. S. Lewis, *The Magicians Nephew* (New York: HarperCollins, 2005), n.p.
10. Alister McGrath, *Glimpsing the Face of God* (Grand Rapids, MI: Wm. B. Eerdmans Publishing, 2002).
11. N. T. Wright, from an audio interview entitled "Reclaiming Worship," © Vineyard Music, USA.
12. Paul Baloche and Graham Kendrick, "Creation's King," © 2005 Integrity's Hosanna! Music, Mobile, AL.

Chapter 4

1. Dr. Dan Allender, "The Hidden Hope in Lament," *Mars Hill Review*, Issue #1, 1994, pp. 25-38.
2. Walter Brueggemann, foreword to Ann Weems, *Psalms of Lament* (Louisville, KY: Westminster John Knox Press, 1995).
3. "The State of Our Nation: A Warning Cry to the People of the United Kingdom," Maranatha Community, Manchester, UK, 2004. http://www.users.zetnet.co.uk/maranathacommunity/documents/state_of_our_nation.pdf (accessed April 2007).
4. Roland Orzabal, "Mad World" © 1982 EMI Virgin Music, Inc., New York.
5. Tim Hughes, "When the Tears Fall," © 2003 Kingsway's Thankyou Music.
6. Ibid.
7. *The American Heritage® Dictionary of the English Language*, Fourth Edition (New York: Houghton Mifflin Company, 2004), s.v. "lament." http://dictionary.reference.com/browse/lament (accessed March 2007).
8. Allender, "The Hidden Hope in Lament."
9. Ibid.

Chapter 5

1. "Did You Know?" *Reader's Digest*, 1997, p. 350.
2. "Fun Toilet Facts," BBC News, November 6, 2005. http://news.bbc.co.uk/cbbcnews/hi/newsid_4390000/newsid_4394200/4394226.stm (accessed March 2007).

3. Helen Briggs, "Sweet Music for Milking," BBC News Online, June 26, 2001. http://news.bbc.co.uk/2/hi/science/nature/1408434.stm (accessed March 2007).

4. "Did You Know?" *Reader's Digest*, 1997, p. 350.

5. Beethoven, quoted in Paul Sullivan, *Sullivan's Music Trivia* (London: Sanctuary Publishing 2003), p. 132.

6. Ibid., p. 57.

7. "Revelers Beware 'Glam Rock Shoulder,'" BBC News Online, December 20, 2000. http://news.bbc.co.uk/1/hi/scotland/1080222.stm (accessed March 2007).

8. William Booth, quoted in "Why Should the Devil Have All the Best Tunes," archived online at the Salvation Army's International Heritage Centre. http://www1.salvationarmy.org/heritage.nsf/0/42d53ced9ec1583080256954004bff3e?OpenDocument (accessed March 2007).

9. Ibid.

10. Alan Light, "Band of the Year: Rock's Unbreakable Heart," *Spin* Magazine, January 2002. http://www.atu2.com/news/article.src?ID=1778 (accessed March 2007).

11. Quoted in Andrew Wilson-Dickson, *The Story of Christian Music* (Minneapolis, MN: Augsburg Fortress Publishers, 2003), p. 60.

12. C. S. Lewis, *The Magicians Nephew* (New York: HarperCollins, 2005), n.p.

13. Matthew Bridges (1852), "Crown Him with Many Crowns."

14. Robert Robinson (1758), "Come Thou Fount of Every Blessing."

Chapter 6

1. Sarah Womack, "How the Pressure to Succeed Is Creating a Generation of Unruly, Depressed Teenagers," *Daily Telegraph*, September 15, 2004. http://www.telegraph.co.uk/global/main.jhtml?xml=/global/2004/09/15/hnteen14.xml (accessed March 2007).

2. Freddie Mercury, quoted at QueenArchives.com. http://www.queenarchives.com/viewtopic.php?t=168 (accessed March 2007).

3. Tim Hughes, "Here I Am to Worship," © 2001 Worshiptogether.com Songs, Brentwood, TN.

Chapter 7

1. "It Must Be True . . . I Read It in the Tabloids," *The Week*, no. 566, June 10, 2006, p. 14.

2. *Amadeus* (1984), written by Peter Shaffer, directed by Milos Forman. http://www.imdb.com/title/tt0086879/ (accessed March 2007).

Chapter 8

1. Bono, keynote address at the fifty-fourth annual National Prayer Breakfast. http://www. americanrhetoric.com/speeches/bononationalprayerbreakfast.htm (accessed March 2007).
2. Richard Foster, *Celebration of Discipline* (London: Hodder and Stoughton, 1989), p. 214.
3. Louie Giglio, *I Am Not but I Know I AM* (Sisters, OR: Multnomah Publishers, Inc., 2005).
4. John Eldredge, *Waking the Dead* (Nashville, TN: Nelson Books, 2003).
5. C. S. Lewis, *The Screwtape Letters* (New York: Harper Collins, 1942), p. 71.
6. Randy Alcorn, "The World Was Not Worthy of Them: Martyrs for Christ." http://www.epm.org/articles/worthy.html (accessed March 2007).
7. John Piper, *Don't Waste Your Life* (Wheaton, IL: Crossway Books, 2003), p. 178.

Closing Thoughts

1. For more information, see www.teamhoyt.com.

Acknowledgments

There were many people involved who made this book possible.

I'm immensely grateful to those who diligently read through various chapters and made insightful and helpful comments—particularly my wife, Rachel (you were amazingly patient and thoughtful, regularly plowing through the manuscript with me late into the night); Mum and Dad; my brothers, Peter and Stephen; Al Gordon and Rob Bewley. Will Jackson—thanks for researching and finding all those great facts!

All those at Kingsway/Survivor, especially Les Moir, Richard Herkes and Carolyn Owen. Thanks for all the hard work you put into this book.

All at Regal Books, especially Bill and Rhonnie Greig and Alex Field. You've constantly encouraged and challenged me to write this book. Thank you for your patience when I continually pushed back the deadline!

Thank you to those leaders, preachers and teachers who have inspired and refined my thinking over the years, my dad, Mike Pilavachi, Nicky Gumbel, Ken Costa, Graham Tomlin, Matt Redman, David Ruis, Don Williams and Louie Giglio.

To my family and friends around the world who faithfully love, support and pray for me.

Tim Hughes is the Dove Award-winning songwriter of "Here I Am to Worship" and is the director of worship at Holy Trinity Brompton in London, England. Tim's other songs include "Beautiful One," "Consuming Fire" and "Name Above All Names." Formerly with Soul Survivor, Tim encourages fellow worshipers from Malaysia to Australia and from South Africa to the United States. He also leads worshipcentral (www.worshipcentral.org), a new school of worship, created to train and equip worship leaders, musicians and worshipers. Worshipcentral is based at Holy Trinity Brompton and run in partnership with Soul Survivor. Tim and his lovely wife, Rachel, live in London.

Also Available in the Best-Selling Worship Series

The Worship God Is Seeking
An Exploration of Worship
and the Kingdom of God
David Ruis
ISBN 978.08307.36928

Blessed be Your Name
Worshipping God on the
Road Marked With Suffering
Matt & Beth Redman
ISBN 978.08307.38199

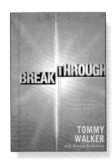

Breakthrough
How to Experience God's Presence
When You Need It Most
Tommy Walker
ISBN 978.08307.39141

The Justice God Is Seeking
Responding to the Heart of God
Through Compassionate Worship
David Ruis
ISBN 978.08307.41977

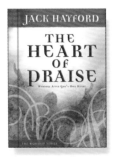

The Heart of Praise
Worship After God's Own Heart
Jack Hayford
ISBN 978.08307.38199

Available at Bookstores Everywhere!

www.regalbooks.com to join **Regal's FREE** e-newsletter. You'll get useful **excerpts from our** est releases and **special access to online chats with your favorite authors.** Sign up today!

Regal
God's Word for Your World™
www.regalbooks.com

Live a Life of Worship

e Unquenchable Worshipper
oming Back to the Heart of Worship
Matt Redman
ISBN 978.08307.29135

The Heart of Worship Files
Featuring Contributions from Some
of Today's Most Experienced
Lead Worshippers
Matt Redman, General Editor
ISBN 978.08307.32616

**I Could Sing of
Your Love Forever**
Stories, Reflections and Devotions
The Worship Series
Delirious?
ISBN 978.08307.43022

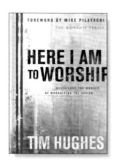

Here I Am to Worship
Never Lose the Wonder
of Worshiping the Savior
Tim Hughes
ISBN 978.08307.33224

Facedown
When You Face Up to God's Glory, You Find
Yourself Facedown in Worship
Matt Redman
ISBN 978.08307.32463

Blessed Be Your Name
Worshipping God on the
Road Marked with Suffering
Matt and Beth Redman
ISBN 978.08307.38193

How Will You Be the Hands and Feet of Jesus?

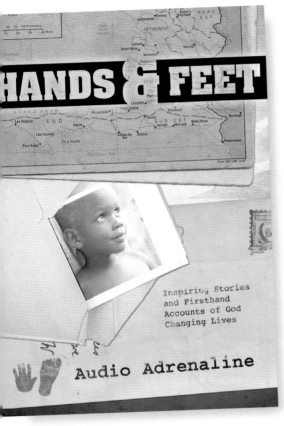

Join Grammy Award-winning Audio Adrenaline deep in the heart of Haiti at The Hands and Feet Project, an orphanage founded by the band members for impoverished children who desperately lack the resources most of us take for granted. Through this travelogue-style journal, full of journal entries and personal stories, you'll discover what it's like to live in the embattled country of Haiti — and how it is possible to change the world, one child at a time.

Hands and Feet
Inspiring Stories and Firsthand
Accounts of God Changing Lives
Audio Adrenaline
ISBN 978.08307.39325

Available at Bookstores Everywhere!

Regal
God's Word for Your World™
www.regalbooks.com